Stars in Your Eyes...

Feet on the Ground

A Practical Guide for Teenage Actors (and their Parents!)

by Annie Jay

with LuAnne Feik

illustrated by Ron Crawford

Theatre Directories
Dorset, Vermont

Theatre Directories is a project of
American Theatre Works, Inc.,
a non-profit 501(c)3 corporation for the performing arts
with offices at 173 Church Street,
P.O. Box 510, Dorset, VT 05251-0510
(802) 867-2223 FAX: (802) 867-0144
E-mail: theatre@sover.net Web page: www.theatredirectories.com

Disclaimer:
A career in the performing arts is an extremely risky venture. Success in this field is a combination of many factors, including: talent, training, determination, contacts, business sense, and a good deal of just plain luck. While the advice given in this book is meant to suggest some starting points for a young actor, there is no guarantee suggested or implied that, simply by following the advice given, a young actor will necessarily succeed. Neither the publisher nor the author accept any responsibility for the outcome of any reader's attempts to follow the advice given here. Likewise, as there is no one "right" way to pursue a career, neither the author nor the publisher represent that the methods described here will work for every person, or that there are not other methods which could work equally well.

Publisher's Cataloging-in-Publication
(Provided by Quality Books, Inc.)

Jay, Annie
    Stars in your eyes-- feet on the ground : a practical guide for teenage actors (and their parents!) / by Annie Jay ; with LuAnne Feik ; illustrated by Ron Crawford. -- 1st ed.
    p. cm.
    Includes index.
    SUMMARY: Provides tips for teenagers seeking to break into the acting profession and avoid scams.
    ISBN: 0-933919-42-5

    1. Acting--Vocational guidance--Juvenile literature. 2. Teenage actors--Vocational guidance. I. Title.
PN2055.J39 1999   792.02'93'0835
                  QBI98-1765

Editor & book design: Jill Charles
Cover design: Ron Crawford
Manufacturing: Daamen Printing, Rutland, Vermont
Printed in the United States of America on acid-free paper
03 02 01 00 99   10 9 8 7 6 5 4 3 2 1

Dedication

To Glenn Kinckner
& Bob Morris,
who discovered me.

Other Publications by Theatre Directories

The Actor's Picture/Resume Book
How to put together a Professional Picture/Resume

Summer Theatre Directory
465 Summer Theatres & Summer Training Programs

Regional Theatre Directory
Jobs & Internships at 430 Regional & Dinner Theatres

Directory of Theatre Training Programs
450 Programs at Colleges, Universities & Conservatories

Student's Guide to Playwriting Opportunities
81 Academic, 105 Developmental Programs for young writers

Auditions and Scenes from Shakespeare
Catalogue of 700 pieces for Monologues and Scene Studies

and see our Special Reports:

- #1. Summer Stock
- #2. Selecting an Undergraduate or Graduate Acting Program
- #3. More about M.F.A. Acting Programs
- #4. Selecting a Training Program in Directing, Playwriting, Design, Tech, or Management
- #5. The Things You Never Learn in College

For more information, or to order any of these books:
Call **1-800-390-2223** or visit our Web site at
www.theatredirectories.com

Table of Contents

Preface

I wish I had wanted to go into the computer or health care field. Magazine headlines and government studies would have confirmed, daily, the wisdom of my decision.

Instead, I have wanted to be a professional actor since fifth grade, when I was the narrator in *Joseph and the Amazing Technicolor Dreamcoat.* Fortunately for me, laughs, applause, and my mother have supported my career choice.

For a young actor, support from parents and guardians is not just nice, it is a necessity. Someone has to drive to auditions, pay for lessons, and understand the pain of rejection.

In a field as competetive as show business, my mother (and co-author) also understood that actors need to begin accumulating professional credits in their teens. Without any contacts in show business, we set out from a Philadelphia suburb to see how far I could get in the theatre, television, and film.

This book is for other young actors and their supporting casts. We hope our script leads to your happy ending, a show business career.

Annie Jay

Introduction

I am one of the kids who was sure I would be discovered–if only the magician had chosen *me* as his helper in a theme park show.

Sad to say, I have learned that staking a professional acting career on the chance of being discovered is like relying on Cinderella's fairy godmother or the Frog Prince's kiss. A young actor's odds of discovery *may* increase in New York and Los Angeles, not because those cities have more Prince Charmings and frog kissers, but because there are more opportunities in these major theatre, film, television, and advertising centers. Those involved in casting a project could like the look or voice of a young person they see at a local restaurant or in the mall. At after-school soccer matches or in a high school musical, students might impress show business moguls who are there to see their own children and grandchildren perform.

But much more often, rather than being discovered through chance contacts, the young actors we see in television sitcoms and commercials, on stage, or on film, got their roles through a standardized casting process. It's a sort of knee-bone-connected-to-the-leg-bone, leg-bone-connected-to-the-ankle-bone sequence: a producer and/or director auditions the performers pre-selected by a casting director. Agents submitted these actors to the casting director because their looks and experience suited the role the casting director described. The agents knew whom to send, because they matched the casting director's descriptions with the actors' resume data in their files.

The actors were on file, because these young performers had found agents willing to represent them. In other words, the actors had successfully auditioned for these agents. They were given the chance to audition, because their professional photos, known as headshots, and the experience, training, and special skills listed on their resumes convinced these agents they were marketable.

Looking at this process, young actors and their parents should realize that show business is competitive, time-consuming, heavy with start-up costs, and subject to chance. It is not a field where you follow a prescribed curriculum, take a certification test, and become a teacher or CPA. It is, however, a field that does have tools, procedures, and pitfalls that young performers can learn. It is also a field much broader than Broadway and Hollywood—a field young performers owe it to themselves to explore.

Stars in your Eyes, Feet on the Ground aims to be a practical guide for talented teens who do not have any special show business connections. It covers the basics: getting a headshot, gaining experience, and writing a resume. The book emphasizes the need to develop a list of industry and media contacts and the importance of sending these contacts frequent mailings publicizing career progress. It touches on a wide range of potential career moves, from beauty pageants to websites; explains union membership; investigates training possibilities, and offers some ways to deal with rejection. Again and again, *Stars in your Eyes, Feet on the Ground* comes back to the young actor's need for parental support. Written especially for parents, Chapter 12 presents a mother's reflections about her daughter's career choice.

Supplementing the text are two appendixes, the first a glossary of terms and the second a list of many helpful resources.

Stars in your Eyes, Feet on the Ground picks up where the thrill of a young actor's first performance ends. I hope it becomes an opening night for many long-running professional acting careers.

Chapter 1: The Supporting Cast

Agents • Personal Managers • Business Managers
Publicists • Parents

A star has a support staff that includes an agent, a personal manager, a business manager, a publicist, and others. I began my acting career with a support staff of one, my mother.

Initially, I needed her help to *flee* the theatre. At age three I spent weeks practicing for my debut in a Montessori Christmas pageant. When I saw the audience on opening night, I decided that I was not quite ready for the pressures of donning my angel wings and singing carols in front of an auditorium packed with parents. My gentle teacher endeavored to coax me to the stage. I wailed in terror, "Don't make me go!" Finally, it was painfully obvious that my teacher was fighting a very lost cause. She handed me over to my mother, who had just found a parking spot in the crowded school lot and had been expecting to enjoy a pleasant evening. Without any recriminations, Mom bundled me into the car, and we returned to our cozy apartment on a cold, wintry night in Green Bay, Wisconsin.

From this inauspicious theatrical beginning, I grew into the role of Traveler One in my final Montessori performance. Mother had to console me, because by then I wanted the lead. When I reached high school, Mom was helping me find auditions, paying for train trips to New York, and writing my news releases. Other beginning actors also must rely on unpaid relatives who are willing and able to donate the kinds of services a star's retinue provides. At the same time, young performers can look ahead. I began to collect the names of agents, managers, and publicists who might be willing to work for me in the future.

Agents represent actors

At the outset, young actors and their families need to perform the functions an agent usually handles. Agents know where the jobs are in theatre, film, television, and advertising. They keep in touch with the casting directors who are buying talent and the actors who are selling their ability to make us laugh and cry. Like a real estate broker who makes a living by knowing who is in the market for a house and which houses are up for sale, agents are show business go-betweens.

Just like homeowners who decide to sell their own homes without paying for a broker's services, young actors can make their own contacts with independent movie producers, community theatres, ad agencies, and others who might hire them directly. In fact, would-be professional performers need to be freelancers who make their own contacts. Agents want young actors with earning power. The more they make, the more agents make from *commissions*, a certain percentage of what actors are paid. It is pretty obvious that an agent does not want to represent someone who has not made any money. Early in their careers, what actors are really doing is auditioning for agents. Every time young actors land roles they become more attractive to agents, because they prove they can generate revenue.

When agents find work for actors, they perform the same functions that employment agencies do. Consequently, agents—and the talent agencies where agents work—are bound by any state licensing, bonding, and other requirements imposed on employment agencies. Agents also are franchised by unions, such as Actors' Equity Association and the Screen Actors Guild. Therefore, they have to abide by union rules and offer union-approved contracts. The way agents make their money is also governed by rules. Actors owe commissions *after* they are cast in a role.

When an agent secures an audition for an actor and the actor lands the role, the actor pays the agent a commission, usually ten percent of gross earnings. Working in their own best interests, agents seek out information about the theatre, television, film, and other projects that need actors. They check *Breakdown Services*, a daily listing of available roles, and they read a variety of trade publications. *Theatrical Index*, for example, gives a weekly casting update for shows on and off-Broadway, as well as for touring companies. *The Hollywood Reporter* provides a similar service for film projects. Both publications are listed in Appendix B.

Even before agents read about roles that might be right for the actors they represent, casting directors may call them. Casting directors, paid by a producer to cast a project, often rely on agents who have helped them by providing the right actors for the right roles in the past. Agents generally try to maintain their can-do reputations. They are not likely to tell a casting director that they do not represent anyone appropriate for a role. At that point, agents may call actors' personal managers for help.

Personal managers can guide careers

Personal managers can recommend their clients to any agent who is submitting actors for an appropriate role. Casting directors also may call managers directly. To help the young actors they have under contract, some personal managers give seminars on show business realities, suggest appearance adjustments and audition material, arrange to make demonstration tapes, offer contract-negotiating strategies, and hound agents to use the actors they manage.

Personal managers, however, do not act as employment agencies, because they do not book actors directly. They work *through* agents, who negotiate contracts and collect their own ten percent commissions on what actors earn. In addition to these agents' commissions, personal managers generally charge the same actors 15 percent commissions for their services. Finding a personal manager with an impeccable reputation is very important, because personal managers are not bound by state employment agency laws, nor are they franchised by any union or covered by any union rules. Whereas an agent is not permitted to conduct business out of his or her home, for example, it is not unusual for managers to use their own homes to interview young actors.

Business managers
look after financial and legal matters

Actors are essentially owner-operated businesses. They require the same type of financial and legal advice as any other entrepreneur. For income tax purposes, young actors need to keep detailed records of and receipts for all work-related expenses, including: headshots; resume and photo printing; postage; travel and parking; subscriptions to professional publications; voice, movement, or acting lessons; agent and manager commissions; and union dues. Come April 15th, these expenses reduce an actor's taxable income. For beginning actors, however, expenses often outrun income, and unfortunately the IRS does not send refunds when deductions total more than earnings.

Beyond what is needed to cover expenses, the young actor needs to set aside money for college, a car, insurance, clothes, and entertainment. When commercial and TV series residuals roll in, actors can begin to think about hiring a business manager and investing in stocks, bonds, and real estate. Until they are 18, actors must rely on parents to handle money responsibly, which includes the parents paying themselves for services provided.

A star's business manager often handles legal as well as financial matters. But in case there is any doubt that even a young actor needs legal help, try reading an agent's or manager's contract. All actors are advised not to work on any project without a written contract. Only when this contract is reviewed by a trusted entertainment attorney does an actor have real peace of mind.

Publicists keep actors in the news

Why does an agent want to represent rock stars, Olympic athletes, sports heroes, movie idols, and beauty pageant winners? Since these people are known and even loved by millions, they bring a readymade audience to any project. Consequently, celebrities command high salaries that translate into high commissions for their agents. Smart actors have learned this lesson from celebrities; they can make themselves more valuable if they hire a publicist to place their names in the news and in feature stories. The more people who know and like an actor, the more she or he will be in demand for a role.

Joanna Pacitti was fired abruptly after she won the national talent search for an Annie to play in the musical's 20th-anniversary Broadway revival. She did not allow herself to become a silent has-been. Her frequent talk-show appearances created an audience for everything she did next: her own dinner-theater revue, *Give My Regards to Broadway*; the New York *Broadway*

Kids Sing Broadway revue; the Aloha Bowl halftime show; playing Annie in a North Carolina regional theatre production. Like I said, smart actors know that their careers require a lifelong publicity campaign.

A young actor's parents play many roles

I am using *parent* to represent guardians, aunts, big brothers, grandmothers, or anyone else a young actor can rely on to do what hired pros do for a star. It is such family members who must help new performers find work, decide on hair styles, choose audition material, handle taxes and finances, understand contracts, and generate a buzz. The publicity buzz is important, because landing a part and giving the best performance in a school musical, at a community theatre, or on a cable TV show can go unnoticed unless someone contacts the media.

The fact that young actors need a supporting cast has many other implications. Parents must have the time, money, energy, desire, and creativity to help their young actors find work. During the Olympics, we hear of young gymnasts and figure skaters who have moved to other cities to train with well-known coaches. Since show business and advertising agencies are concentrated in New York and Los Angeles, the serious young actor also needs to leave home for these centers frequently, if not permanently. There is no question that the family's life will be disrupted. Often, the whole family cannot go with the actor, because a parent's work simply may not permit relocation. The central question is how families will react to long separations and to the attention focused on one member.

Mom and the young actor might make trips to auditions, the way Brooke Shields, Ricky Schroder, and Jodi Foster did with their moms. Heading for the car, Mom innocently asks, "Do you have your headshot?" Whether the response is a tirade, silence, or a simple, "Yes," Mom has to remain calm. No one wants to blow an opportunity because parent and child get on each other's nerves.

Recognizing that the young performer is under pressure requires a mature parent who knows how to establish an understanding, often humorous relationship. Parent and child have to be compatible over long periods of time. An early-morning appointment can mean staying at a hotel the night before an audition. Travel always requires patience. Glitches in plans and timetables are normal. Travelers can expect to get stuck in traffic on a turnpike or circling an airport in an airplane. Waiting for an audition or for take after take during a commercial or film becomes an art form in itself.

One time-killer my Mom and I created is a game we call "Going to Poughkeepsie for Popcorn." Progressing through the alphabet letter by letter, we took turns coming up with different locations and items, the more unusual the better. On airplane trips, we made hand puppets out of barf bags and played cards and travel-sized Scrabble. At a beauty pageant, we blocked out a runway area in a parking lot after seeing the hotel ballroom where the final competition would be held. Waiting time was spent moving over asphalt, waving, turning, and smiling at the invisible judges.

Parents can use their experienced eyes and ears to help, or their actions can undermine success and psyches. On the one hand, they can size up the competition, keep the mood light, and help process the constant flow of information. For example, in some audition settings, what goes on with performers who precede you is remarkably easy to hear even though doors are closed. If the actor ahead of you is loud, a supportive parent can point out tactfully that this probably is not the right approach for conversational, reality-based commercials.

On the other hand, undisciplined parents can destroy an actor's confidence and self-esteem, and make enemies of the staff one is trying to impress. Not unlike disappointed parents at a Little League game, when a performance fails to satisfy expectations, moms and dads have been known to scold young actors in public. They also can fuss too much with a young actor's hair and clothes, bother those who are running an audition, and aggravate agents by whining about scheduling.

Family and friends have to be there with comfort and understanding when young actors have nothing to show for time, money, and preparations devoted to a project. Mother and I learned to take disappointments in stride. Two in New York come to mind. We took a train up to the city one Saturday, when I was supposed to audition for a student film. No one was at the assigned location, and no one answered the telephone number I had been given. Then again, I wish no one *had* been at my first New York audition for a musical. Mother read my face as soon as I emerged from the audition room. She knew we had to make a hasty retreat before I broke into tears. Instead of waiting for an elevator, we headed for the stairs. Confidence restored, I have since auditioned in New York for another musical. I still did not get the part, but I made it through two callbacks.

As volunteer P. T. Barnums, parents are not finished when their young actors land callbacks, commercials, theatrical roles, or film parts. While a star can hire a publicist to distribute news releases and publicity photos to the media, with young actors that task falls to parents, along with their other jobs as wardrobe assistants, tax consultants, and designated drivers. My mother developed a newsletter (Figs. 1 & 2, pages 9 & 10) for me the way a fan club would create one for a star. Sent to agents, managers, and the media, my newsletter gives me a recognizable format to reinforce my image over and over again in the show business market.

Fig. 1: An issue of my Newsletter

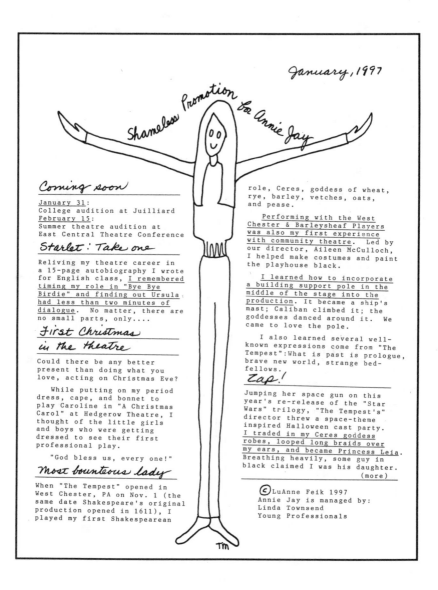

January, 1997

Shameless Promotion for Annie Jay

Coming soon

January 31:
College audition at Juilliard
February 15:
Summer theatre audition at
East Central Theatre Conference

Starlet: Take one

Reliving my theatre career in
a 15-page autobiography I wrote
for English class, I remembered
timing my role in "Bye Bye
Birdie" and finding out Ursula
had less than two minutes of
dialogue. No matter, there are
no small parts, only....

First Christmas in the theatre

Could there be any better
present than doing what you
love, acting on Christmas Eve?

While putting on my period
dress, cape, and bonnet to
play Caroline in "A Christmas
Carol" at Hedgerow Theatre, I
thought of the little girls
and boys who were getting
dressed to see their first
professional play.

"God bless us, every one!"

Most bounteous lady

When "The Tempest" opened in
West Chester, PA on Nov. 1 (the
same date Shakespeare's original
production opened in 1611), I
played my first Shakespearean
role, Ceres, goddess of wheat,
rye, barley, vetches, oats,
and pease.

Performing with the West
Chester & Barleysheaf Players
was also my first experience
with community theatre. Led by
our director, Aileen McCulloch,
I helped make costumes and paint
the playhouse black.

I learned how to incorporate
a building support pole in the
middle of the stage into the
production. It became a ship's
mast; Caliban climbed it; the
goddesses danced around it. We
came to love the pole.

I also learned several well-
known expressions come from "The
Tempest":What is past is prologue,
brave new world, strange bed-
fellows.

Zap!

Jumping her space gun on this
year's re-release of the "Star
Wars" trilogy, "The Tempest's"
director threw a space-theme
inspired Halloween cast party.
I traded in my Ceres goddess
robes, looped long braids over
my ears, and became Princess Leia.
Breathing heavily, some guy in
black claimed I was his daughter.
(more)

©LuAnne Feik 1997
Annie Jay is managed by:
Linda Townsend
Young Professionals

Fig. 2: The back of my Newsletter

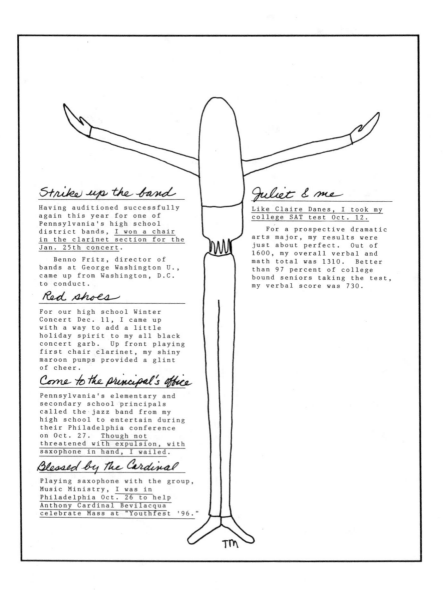

Strike up the band

Having auditioned successfully again this year for one of Pennsylvania's high school district bands, I won a chair in the clarinet section for the Jan. 25th concert.

Benno Fritz, director of bands at George Washington U., came up from Washington, D.C. to conduct.

Red shoes

For our high school Winter Concert Dec. 11, I came up with a way to add a little holiday spirit to my all black concert garb. Up front playing first chair clarinet, my shiny maroon pumps provided a glint of cheer.

Come to the principal's office

Pennsylvania's elementary and secondary school principals called the jazz band from my high school to entertain during their Philadelphia conference on Oct. 27. Though not threatened with expulsion, with saxophone in hand, I wailed.

Blessed by the Cardinal

Playing saxophone with the group, Music Ministry, I was in Philadelphia Oct. 26 to help Anthony Cardinal Bevilacqua celebrate Mass at "Youthfest '96."

Juliet & me

Like Claire Danes, I took my college SAT test Oct. 12.

For a prospective dramatic arts major, my results were just about perfect. Out of 1600, my overall verbal and math total was 1310. Better than 97 percent of college bound seniors taking the test, my verbal score was 730.

Chapter 2: Props

Picture/Resume • Postcards • Demonstration Tape

       If any rite of passage marks the transition from talented amateur to professional actor, it is the process of creating your picture/resume, or "headshot." Known as the industry's business card, the headshot introduces a young actor to agents, managers, and casting directors—to the world of show business. At open calls, where anyone can audition for a part, actors may be asked to line up and, one after another, present their headshots. Once the audition's over, the headshots remain behind to remind everyone that your eyes sparkle and you could be perfect for the part.

Your look, your headshot

A headshot is an 8-inch by 10-inch professional black and white photo of your face. It has to look exactly like you, the person who will turn up for an audition. That means, before beginning the search for a professional photographer, you have to like all the features that you observe when you look in a mirror. Should you see a blond, clear-eyed, clear-skinned stunner who resembles Alicia Silverstone or Leonardo DiCaprio, you are in demand, as is. Head straight for a photographer. A modeling agency or shopping network might even be willing to look at your snapshot collection and sign you before your professional proofs dry.

Most of us have room for improvement, though. Start at the top: Do you need a new haircut, style or color? Should you see a dermatologist? Do your eyebrows need plucking? If your eyes are usually puffy in the morning, remember to schedule an afternoon photo session. If you tend to look like you need an afternoon nap, your photo shoot must be before noon. Since eyes are a prime consideration to those who do the casting, young women should start to figure out ways to bring out this feature with a bit of makeup.

As a rule, all women should wear some makeup for a photo shoot. The camera is going to pick up light and shadow playing across the bumps and planes of any face unless at least a foundation base helps smooth skin texture and cover any unsightly blemishes. Leave exposed, however, a sprinkling of freckles or a well-placed mole. Young men can generally rely on their photographer, who will have a supply of powder to take off shine, or foundation to cover a blemish, as needed.

Cosmetics are applied differently for a photo shoot than for everyday wear. Contrast, not color, is important in black and white photos. Blush applied lower than normal will help accent lighter cheekbones. Eyeliner, too noticeably unnatural if it is dark and defined, enhances the eyes when applied by brush with a delicate touch. Try some experiments, and ask a friend to take black and white photos of the results. If you still feel insecure about your skills, professional help from a cosmetic company's department store beauty advisor is *not* the answer. Instead, ask your photographer to recommend a professional makeup artist. It will be easy to justify the extra $75 to $150 added to the cost of the shoot, the first time you are called to audition for a television commercial.

My major problem was yellow teeth no makeup could hide. How could I flash a dazzling smile when my teeth made me self-conscious? My dentist told me there was a safe whitening process that took only a few weeks. After making an impression of my upper teeth, he gave me a mold that I filled with a solution and wore for an hour each day after school. The process was repeated for my bottom teeth. Although not inexpensive, the technique was fast, painless, and effective.

Dressing for black and white photographic success also relies on contrasts. Tanned redheads in green sweaters may look wonderful in person, but a black and white photograph picks up only uninteresting shades of gray. To gather clues about what makes great photos, I looked through a book devoted to "Best Actress" Oscar winners. In these black and white photos, Elizabeth Taylor and Vivien Leigh stood out with their black hair and pale skins. Blonds, like Ingrid Bergman, Meryl Streep, and Julie Christie, emphasized their eyes. Lipsticks varied. Some used dark; some, light. Brunette Katharine Hepburn wore her hair in a mass of curls and waves, defined her eyes, and kept lips pale. Satin, chiffon, and velvet photographed particularly well on movie stars. Light-colored clothes predominated.

Photographers prefer that we stay away from pure white and black outfits, because these cause lighting and contrast headaches. Necklines require some experimentation. Try on round necks, v-necks, layered shirts and sweaters, blouses and blazers, denim jackets over tank tops, open and closed collars. I have been told that my favorite turtleneck hides too much to look good in a headshot. In general, headshot "rules" dictate that we stay away from anything that detracts from our faces:

jewelry, strong patterns, fussy ruffles, hats, and—unless they are worn to every audition—glasses.

Outfits can project your type: upscale preppy, clean-cut "all-American," cute, funky, sophisticated, outdoor jock, smoldering leading man, tough guy, innocent ingenue. Decide which way or ways you want to go. You will be able to change clothes and pose in several outfits during one photo session. At home, try changing positions in each outfit that you plan to wear. This way, you can avoid bringing any clothes that cause problems. You do not want to undermine your relaxed, natural, alive expression by worrying about straightening unbecoming folds or reclosing a button after every shot.

Another key to looking relaxed is to *be* relaxed. Unclutter your mind by assembling everything you plan to take to the photographer's studio before the last minute. All outfits should be ready to go in a cleaning or garment bag. I keep a list of all the other items I might need to take with me. On the day of a shoot, I can just put them in a carrying pouch without agonizing about whether or not I am forgetting something. I have found that I can leave the list in the pouch as a ready reminder of what I need to take on auditions, trips, and sleep overs. My list includes a hairbrush, hair spray, contact lens fluid, lipstick, shine-covering powder, a toothbrush, and toothpaste.

More choices: Headshot or portrait?

While the headshot was standard for many years, actors today may opt for photos that show them from head to waist, hips, knees, or even feet. This more inclusive portrait style is sometimes referred to as a "three-quarters shot" (indicating that the photo shows more than a face and neckline, not that it shows three-quarters of the face).

Portrait photos, often taken outside in natural light rather than in a studio, might show an actor sitting on a rock or casually leaning against a wall. Those casting for the theatre, or those interested in what type of character an actor projects on television or film, might like to see more than just a face. If such a photo would flatter you, plan to have both headshots and portrait photos taken at the same session. Any photographer should be able to satisfy your request by pulling the camera back a few feet to switch from headshots to portraits.

When the process was new to me, I set out to find a photographer who could come up with one great headshot. The beginning actor has no need to pay more for a "composite," a sheet of several pictures showing different looks. Composites are used to book print advertising and other modeling jobs, but they are not the industry norm for theatre, television, and film work. In other words, even though you posed in different clothes with different expressions at your photo shoot, you will select only one picture for your headshot.

To find a photographer, you can contact any local direct mail and catalogue companies, newspapers, magazines, theatrical and modeling agencies, professional theatres, and advertising agencies to see if these organizations are willing to recommend the professionals they use. If the only available photographic studios concentrate on wedding photos and executive portraits for corporate newsletters, so be it. My first headshot was taken by a wedding photographer three blocks from my home (see Fig. #3, page 25). Using that picture, I was hired to play the lead in a student film at New York University.

After compiling a list of potential photographers, the next step is for you and your parent to visit their studios, look through their portfolios at samples of their work, and see if you are comfortable talking to them and their assistants. You will want to ask about costs, how soon you can see proofs, and how long it will take to get your 8"x10" prints. If you are using a local photographer instead of a professional theatrical photographer, you should explain that you need an 8"x10" black and white photo of your face that clearly shows your features. No matter how a photographer asks you to position your head, hands, and body during a shoot, remember to look straight into the camera lens. You definitely do not want a dramatic, Barrymore-like profile. Shadows that obscure parts of your face, latticework sets, and pastoral backgrounds are out.

Some photographers offer package deals; other have separate sitting fees and prices for photo prints. Retouching to remove under-the-eye shadows or a flyaway hair adds extra charges. A professional theatrical photographer could be expected to charge between $175 and $350 to cover the sitting fee for shooting three rolls of film, or 108 shots, and making two or three prints. Nontheatrical photographers usually take far fewer shots; the local wedding photographer I used took only ten. The most recent photographer I used offered a special young actor's rate that included 8"x10" prints of four different poses. I used the three extra photos for gifts.

All young female and male actors can gain confidence about their photo sessions by studying *The Actor's Picture/Resume Book* listed in Appendix B. One of the most useful bits of advice co-author and photographer Tom Bloom provides is his suggestion to *think about a secret you want to share* as you are being photographed.

Posing for amateur snapshots is always good practice. I have a cousin who never takes a bad family photo. She learned as a toddler to look towards her mother's camera and smile. You will find examples of good expressions, makeup, shirts, lighting, printing, and cropping in *The Actor's Picture/Resume Book*. Start looking closely at photos in magazines and catalogues, too, and you will find many more.

When you receive your contact sheets, or proofs, with up to 108 little you's looking back, do not pressure yourself to make a hasty decision about which photo, whether a headshot or portrait, will represent you. Ask the photographer to lend you a magnifier, or *loupe*, and examine each photo separately, preferably at home. Eliminate the worst, and look for the ones where your eyes are wide open and alive.

A resume answers the question, "What have you done?"

A one-page resume gives agents, managers, and casting directors your vital statistics, tells them what you have done, and suggests what your training and special skills have prepared you to do in the future.

The easy part is centering your name and listing your union memberships, if any, your height and weight, and your hair and eye colors. You want to make sure that everyone casting a role knows how to get in touch with you, but you do not want to print your home telephone number and address on your resume. As my manager says, "There are too many crazies out there." The solution is investing in a pager or an answering service and in a box at the post office or a local package mailing store. On your resume, you can list one or more of the following contact numbers for: a pager, a telephone service, a telephone answering machine with a businesslike message, a fax machine, your agent's or manager's telephone and fax. You can use your post office box number in return address labels on your mailings (no address should be printed on the resume).

Actors under 18 should state their birth dates; this advises a director that they are subject to child labor laws, such as the number of hours a day they can work, what time their work day must end, and state requirements for work permits, schooling, and supervision. Older actors should not list their ages. Some in the cast of *Beverly Hills 90210* were "high school students" in their 30s. Short and youthful-looking New York actress Jennifer Dundas was 26 when she played a 16-year-old in *Good as New* and 17-year-old Alexandra in a revival of *The Little Foxes*. Clothing sizes are unnecessary. If there's any question about your citizenship, you should include your official status with the U.S. Immigration & Naturalization Service.

Filling in the sections for experience, training, and special skills on your resume will motivate you to look for opportunities to audition and take classes.

When you are just starting your career, you will list parts in school plays and church pageants as credits (See Fig. 4, page 26.) This early background will drop off of your resume as your experience accumulates—as you add credits from professional theatre, film, television, and commercials. Dates of your performances should not be included.

Aim for a clean, uncluttered look. Help casting directors focus on the roles you have played or understudied in various plays, films, and television shows; where you performed; stations that aired your performances; and who your directors were. As you build up more credits, you will be able to create separate categories, such as regional theatre, dinner theatre, summer stock productions, and eventually off-Broadway and Broadway. Ideally, you should prepare a number of different resumes for different types of work. If you are trying out for a film role, list your film experience first. If you want to be considered for a play, list your theatre experience first, and so on. But whichever category you choose to emphasize, within each category your resume should list your most impressive credits first, rather than chronologically.

In *Acting as a Business*, a reference listed in Appendix B, Brian O'Neil stresses the importance of mentioning callbacks on your resume. That you have been called back to a second or third audition, even if you did not ultimately get the part, suggests a level of professionalism. It shows that you know how to audition successfully.

O'Neil's book also provides useful advice about how to handle commercials on your resume. Actors cannot be principals in current commercials for competing companies, such as Coke and Pepsi. Even when their commercials are no longer running, actors are often afraid that they will not be considered by competing advertisers, if they list sponsors by name on their resumes. To avoid broadcasting a real or apparent conflict of interest, under "Commercials," actors often print, "Conflicts upon request." As O'Neil points out, actors who have never done commercials have been known to use the same wording on their resumes. That is why he suggests that those who have made commercials should use the wording, "Tape upon request," to show that they are willing to offer proof of their experience. The tape supplied can show clearly which commercials are airing currently and which have run in the past.

In a resume's "Training" section, agents and casting directors expect to see entries such as acting, voice (indicating vocal range), dance, speech, and on-camera technique. Your hope is to have trained with someone whose name an agent or casting director will recognize and respect. No matter how many academic honors you have won or how high your grades and SAT scores, examples of your intellectual brilliance have no place in any section of a theatrical resume. You can feature your academic accomplishments on the different resume you use to apply for non-theatrical summer and after-school positions.

Ending a resume with the "Special Skills" section provides insight into a young actor's unique personality. This is the place to talk about athletic abilities, language and juggling skills, stage combat and musical instrument training, and whether or not you can drive a car. Watch what young people are doing in current commercials to spot skills in demand. If you have those skills and you perform them expertly, list them.

Preparing picture/resumes and postcards

Once you have a headshot and resume, you are ready to look for representation by an agent and manager, to attend open calls, and to respond to casting notices published in your local newspaper or a trade paper, such as *Back Stage* (one of the publications listed in Appendix B). Incidentally, when a notice asks you to send a headshot, the casting director actually expects to see a picture and a resume. That also goes for auditions. "Bring a headshot," really means, "Bring a picture/resume."

To take advantage of every show business opportunity, both your headshot and resume have to be reproduced in quantity. The reproduction houses listed in Appendix B produce multiple prints of your headshot for about 50¢ each. Since photographers usually keep the negative of your 8"x10" print, reproduction companies will charge to make another negative, which they will return to you for future use.

You may find that one company offers 500 headshots for what another charges for half that number. Different processes probably explain the price difference. Less expensive *lithographic* prints, such as you see in books or newspapers, are produced from negatives composed of dots (clusters of many for black and fewer for gray). More expensive *photographic* prints have a sharper image produced by chemicals that cause photographic paper to pick up every tone from white to black. For a first impression, I feel more confident presenting a high-quality photographic print. Casting people look at dozens of headshots at the same time, and I want mine to stand out, sharp and clear.

When you contact reproduction houses by mail or telephone, ask them to send you samples, as well as a price list and order form. You will see that companies provide various alternatives: prints with white borders, no borders, different typefaces for printing your name, glossy, semi-gloss, or matte finishes. Headshot fads come and go, and it seems the 8"x10" glossy is out. The 8"x10" matte finish is now preferred.

You do not have to have your name printed on your headshot, but it is a way to help agents and casting directors associate your name and face. On a borderless print, your name can be printed in black on a light area or in white, known as "reverse," on a darker area of your sweater or jacket. Another popular headshot style includes a wide white border where your name, union affiliations, and/or agent/manager contact information can be printed in black. As for type styles for printing your name, surveys show that most agents and casting directors prefer a newspaper-style "serif" typeface—one with short cross lines at the ends of each letter, like the typeface used here.

Reproduction houses can print your resume on the back of your headshot, but I have found that my show business career is in too much flux to merit such a permanent record. Consider just two examples from the sample resumes on pages 26 and 28. In a period of eighteen months, I gained a manager, and went from mentioning callbacks at Hedgerow Theatre to listing several parts I played there. Also, if you have separate resumes for film, television, theatre, and commercials, printing these different versions on the backs of your headshots does not make sense. You could end up with too many for film and not enough for theatre. The best idea is to attach resumes to headshots as needed.

Expect to print new resumes on a computer whenever your credits change. Some suggest copying resumes on off-white or light gray paper to reduce the glare for those examining them under bright office lights. Remember when printing a resume on 8 1/2"x11" paper to keep copy within the 8"x10" area of your headshot. Then, before or after stapling or pasting the four corners of your resume back-to-back with your headshot, trim your resume to 8"x10" (a paper trimmer from an office supply store is a good investment).

To mail picture/resumes, actors need basic supplies: 9"x12" envelopes, stationery, return address labels, paper clips, and stamps. Using a paper clip, attach a sheet of paper (a stand-in for your cover letter) to your picture/resume and put these pieces in your envelope. It is not necessary to include a cardboard support. Ask the post office to tell you how much postage you need on your envelopes, and buy a supply of stamps to have on hand for future mailings.

For every picture/resume you send, take time to write a cover letter, whether by hand or on a computer or typewriter. In two or three sentences, say that you would like to audition for a particular part and why your look and experience make you perfect for that role. When writing to potential agents or managers, state clearly that you would like their representation, call attention to the experience and training listed on your resume, and mention any referral—someone they know who has given you their name.

One mailing is never enough. What publicists do to keep famous stars in the headlines, you have to do for yourself. After sending a picture/resume, many actors follow up with photo postcards that tell agents, managers and casting directors about new roles they have landed and suggest they be considered for future projects. You should also consider doing this. The same reproduction houses that print headshots also print postcards, and you can have your headshot reproduced on 100 or more photo postcards right away. Another option is to wait until you have a publicity photo from one of your performances. After all, what better way is there to impress an agent with the fact that you are working than to send a photo postcard showing you in costume and in action?

Snapshots of performances will not do, however. Somehow you have to find a way to have a professional photographer produce a high-quality print of your performance photo. I was lucky when a local newspaper ran an article about my stint as a "Phanstormer" at Phillies' baseball games. I called the paper to get a copy of the photo its photographer took to run with the feature and then had it reproduced as a postcard. To the agents I had been courting, I wrote the following note on the back:

As a "Phanstormer," I am entertaining at Philadelphia Phillies' home games this summer. If a part calls for a female athlete or funny improv, I've played that role. As of Oct. 1, I'll be living in NYC. — Annie Jay

It was during my six months with the Phillies that I found that I had real improv talent—I could relate to people and act without a script. To feature this skill, I added an "Improv" section to my resume. My experience in this area of my resume would expand, when I worked as a Christmas elf helping Santa at Macy's.

Demonstration tapes can audition anywhere

In my sophomore year of high school, I learned that I did not have all the props I needed to pursue an acting career. The scholarship application for a state-sponsored, summer arts program required an audition on videotape. A friend who was auditioning for a voice scholarship was asked to submit an audiotape. Subsequently, I found that summer theatre internships and college scholarship applications also required me to submit demonstration tapes. In the professional world, agents and managers on one coast regularly send "demo" tapes across the country to the other, as soon as they hear of parts perfect for the actors they represent. As a television sportscaster, my half-brother auditions by sending videotapes to stations throughout the country.

I can imagine, some time during my anticipated forty- or fifty-year show business career, that the industry will make the short hop from demos to an Internet-driven casting system. The faster computer terminals can download audio and video clips, the easier it will be for agents, managers, and casting directors to click on Web sites where actors run their commercials, film excerpts, monologues, and song and dance routines.

Until online casting replaces the exchange of cassettes, the demo will continue to be one more important start-up expense a young actor needs to consider. Unfortunately, you cannot take a camcorder to the basement or a tape recorder to your bedroom and produce a competitive demo. My mother called a local cable television station to see if anyone at the studio could help me prepare a professional tape for the summer arts program. Chalking it up as community service, the station volunteered to assist me this one time for free. I arrived at the studio, rehearsed with the cameraman, and recorded a "slate," an introduction stating my name and the role I would enact. Then I did several takes of the same monologue. We transferred the slate and my best performance to a videotape that I entered in the scholarship competition.

The next time I needed a taped audition, I asked my manager to recommend a studio. At my scheduled time, I taped several versions of two monologues. My slate and the two best performances were combined onto one cassette for $330. For $7 per cassette, East Coast Video (see "Sources" in Appendix B) duplicated the original on 1/2" VHS cassettes. Singers and dancers also may need studios to help them prepare the taped musical accompaniment they may be asked to bring to their auditions.

Experienced actors usually make one demo with their commercials and another with clips from film and television appearances. In as little as five minutes, careful editing can capture an actor's best scenes, display her range, and develop a rhythm that presents a performer at her best. Accomplished singers, musicians, and those who do cartoon character voices, accents, and dialects or read dialogue for voice-overs demonstrate their skills on audio cassettes no more than three minutes long. In all cases, demo tapes make a forceful, concise statement about talent and experience.

With your demo in hand, you now have the props you need to audition for appropriate roles being cast anywhere in the world.

Fig. 3: My first headshot

Annie Jay

Fig. #4: An early resume

ANNIE JAY

Date of birth: May 3, 1979
Height: 5/4"
Weight: 112 lbs.
Hair: Brown
Eyes: Blue

Telephone: 610-XXX-XXXX
Fax: 610-XXX-XXXX

THEATRE

PINOCCIO	Catnip Kate the Cat	Missoula Children's Theatre
AH, WILDERNESS!	aud. for Muriel , 2 callbacks	Hedgerow Theatre Dir: Penelope Reed

FIILM

THE SHACK	Mary (lead)	NYU thesis film Dir: Leila Godowsky
Philadelphia Teacher's Retirement Fund	School girl	Industrial film Dir: Shawn Campbell

SCHOOL PLAYS

ANNIE	Miss Hannigan	H.S. for Creative and
BYE BYE, BIRDIE	Ursula	Performing Arts, Phila.
OLLIVER!	The Artful Dodger	

TRAINING

Acting:	Improvisation, West Chester University H.S. for Creative and Performing Arts, Philadelphia
Voice:	Darlington Fine Arts Center with L. Thomas (soprano)
Tap and Jazz:	West Chester Performing Arts Center with Gail Oldfield and Myra Bazell
Clarinet and Saxophone:	Dragonetti Studio with Dave Withowski

SPECIAL SKILLS

German, French and Cockney accents; clarinet, saxophone; drive car (automatic); figure skating, riding a bicycle, softball, volleyball, swimming; great with animals.

Fig. 5: My recent headshot

Fig. #6: A more recent resume

ANNIE JAY
Equity Membership Candidate
Beatty Management • Phone 301-XXX-XXXX • Fax 301-XXX-XXXX

Height: 5/4"
Weight: 112 lbs.

Hair: Brown; Eyes: Blue
Vocal Range: Soprano

THEATRE

Hedgerow Theatre, PA (Resident Company)

A CHRISTMAS CAROL	Belle	Dir: Zoran Kovcic
THE UNINVITED	Stella Meredith	Dir: Janet Kelsey
THE GOOD DOCTOR	Julia	Dir: Josh Browns
MARAT/SADE	Nun	Dir: Penelope Reed
SABOTAGE IN SPACE	Cheerleader Bridesmaid	SoulStar (tour), Dir: Vito Settineri
REBECCA	Maid	American Stage Festival, NH
		Dir: Matthew Parent
THE TEMPEST	Ceres	Barleysheaf Theatre, PA
	Ariel (u/s)	Dir: Aileen McCulloch

THEATRE FOR YOUNG AUDIENCE

HOUSE AT POOH CORNER	Piglet	Amer. Stage Fest., Dir: Francene Zahra
RAMONA QUIMBY	Old Woman	Dir: Elizabeth Wolf
PINOCCIO	Catnip Kate the Cat	Missoula Children's Theatre

IMPROV

Phanstormer	Philadelphia Phillies, Veterans Stadium	Dir: Joe Ranoia
Christmas Elf	Macy's Department Store, NYC	Dir: Jim Dowd

FIILM

THE SHACK	Mary (lead)	NYU thesis film, Dir: Leila Godowsky
PATRICK	Mental Patient	NYU thesis film
	(featured role)	Dir: Jeffrey Morgan
A PLEASANT SHADE OF GRAY	Bar patron	Independent film, Dir: James Gardiner
Teacher's Retirement Fund	School girl	Industrial film, Dir: Shawn Campbell

TRAINING

Acting, Improvisation:	West Chester University
	H.S. for Creative and Performing Arts, Philadelphia
Voice:	Darlington Fine Arts Center with L. Thomas
Dance (Tap & Jazz):	Gail Oldfield and Myra Bazell
Clarinet & Saxophone:	Dragonetti Studio with Dave Withowski

SPECIAL SKILLS

German, French, Cockney and Standard British accents; clarinet, saxophone; drive car (automatic); figure skating, softball, volleyball, swimming; great with animals & children.

Chapter 3: Making the Rounds

Database • Mailings • News Release • Media Kits

To find work and representation, young actors need to become known and liked as talented performers. Such recognition requires contacts. I began collecting the names of those who should receive my headshot and news of career progress on 3"x5" index cards. Separated with dividers for Agents, Personal Managers, Business Managers, etc., these cards were filed in a box that once contained the nouns and verbs I needed to memorize for an advanced German class. Now I was creating a file of people who I hoped would memorize *my* name. Eventually I transferred the names in my file box to computer files.

Build a personal database

Successful actors pay attention to principles that guide the direct mail business. Compare a personal letter, hand addressed to someone by name, with an envelope carrying a mass-produced label sent to Resident or Current Occupant. The lesson is clear. Picture/resumes and all other mailings have to be sent to individuals, preferably in hand-addressed envelopes.

How to find names of agents and managers

My database began with a single manager's name, a woman recommended by a friend of my aunt. My mother called her when I sang the lead in our fifth-grade musical. She said to send a headshot, which I did not have at the time. Through the years, Mom finally did send picture/resumes, newsletters, and news releases. Seven years later, the woman who had been the first name in my index file became my personal manager.

I began to collect other database names and addresses by looking for agents in our local telephone book. Although I include telephone numbers in my file, agents usually tell performers to make contacts by mail. They want to keep their telephone lines open for casting directors looking for the actors they represent. In Philadelphia's *Yellow Pages*, I found 14 listings under "Theatrical Agencies." A couple were acting schools, but it was a start.

I also looked under "Labor Organizations," because I once read a newspaper article that said the Screen Actors Guild (SAG) and the American Federation of Television & Radio Artists (AFTRA) were willing to send their franchised agency lists to anyone who mailed them a stamped, self-addressed, business-size envelope. In Philadelphia, both entertainment unions shared the same address. Responding to my request, SAG sent not only a list of its franchised agents in the Philadelphia area but also a list of independent casting directors who work with these agents.

Moving beyond the Philadelphia area, I sent a money order for $3.00, payable to Screen Actors Guild, and a self-addressed, stamped business envelope to SAG's national headquarters in Los Angeles (see Appendix B). The list I received identified union franchised agencies in 26 cities. Like the one in Philadelphia, other SAG branch offices listed in Appendix B may provide additional information about local independent casting directors who are willing to audition freelance actors not represented by agents. Some SAG listings also indicate which agencies specialize in representing children, teens, dancers, actors from specific ethnic backgrounds, and people with disabilities.

What these listings do *not* do is identify individual contacts within the agencies. In some cases, the name of the agency is the name of the key contact, but it is better to call the firm and ask who should receive your picture/resume mailing. The New York manager credited with discovering the young Tom Cruise told me that New York agents do not like to work with actors who live more than an hour away from Manhattan. Travel time, therefore, may limit, initially, the number of agents' names that make it into your file box or computer files. Since I planned to move to Manhattan as soon as I finished high school, I included agents from Philadelphia and New York in my file.

Concentrations of agents in New York City and the Los Angeles area indicate that the greatest amount of work in theatres, commercials, television, film, and modeling can be found in these localities. Month after month, the *Ross Reports Television & Film* publication (see Appendix B) provides a detailed list of everyone involved in casting projects in New York and California.

In some agencies listed in *Ross Reports Television & Film*, a picture/resume mailed to one agent will be circulated to everyone in the agency. In other agentices, however, a picture/resume will go only to the agent to whom it is addressed. Unless a telephone call can determine which is a firm's procedure, an actor interested in appearing in commercials, for example, is faced with a choice: sending a cover letter and headshot to each agent that *Ross Reports Television & Film* lists under "Commercials," or picking one agent per firm and hoping for the best. One further complication: agents and agencies are constantly changing. It is necessary to compare your file entries with each new monthly issue of *Ross Reports.*

Rather than hunting down names of agents, young actors who live away from major cities may create a database with a slightly different orientation. For the immediate future, it could be more productive to find out who is hiring print models for local department stores, actors for local television commercials, interns for a nearby theatre, extras for a summer pageant, and children to be part of families cast in a local corporation's industrial-training film. Experience in these professional venues adds real value to a young performer's resume, even more than playing the lead in the school play.

In a small town or major metropolitan area, young actors can find names to add to their databases and stay on top of show business developments simply by reading daily newspapers, magazines, and entertainment trade papers. Even if you do not subscribe to *Back Stage,* one of the periodicals in Appendix B, remind yourself to order the annual "Kids in Show Biz" issue that the paper publishes the first week in April. The bulk of the manager names in my database came from one of these issues. Just by reading the newspaper, Mom and I have learned that Elaine Goldsmith-Thomas is Julia Robert's agent and that Caresse Norman is Madonna's manager. Both Goldsmith-Thomas and Norman are now in my files. We also read about Mike Burg, Tara Lipinski's agent and a likely file entry for actors who are skilled figure skaters.

Identify potential
business managers and legal counsel

Compared with my list of over a hundred agents and personal managers, my files of business managers and entertainment attorneys are slim. Right now in the financial area, my major problem is making enough income to offset the show-business-related expenses that I would like to deduct on my income tax form. This will be true for most young actors. Fortunately, I have a cousin who is a Certified Public Accountant willing to help me when I start making a bundle.

To fill my legal file, I called the Bar Association in Philadelphia. As in other cities and states, this organization has a lawyer referral and information service that can supply the names of attorneys who specialize in entertainment law. Under the service's auspices, an initial consultation in Philadelphia costs $25. I also have found names of lawyers by looking through my parents' alumni magazines and listing law-school graduates who went into the field of entertainment law. All actors should include in their files the telephone hotline number, listed in Appendix B, of the Volunteer Lawyers for the Arts. This organization stands ready to provide quick answers to arts-related legal questions.

Cultivate media contacts

Until they can hire publicists to turn their names into household words, young actors have to handle their own media contacts. If I want to convince an agent or casting director that an audience will pay to see me, I have to start building a portfolio of articles and a tape of interviews and appearances showing that people have heard of me. I cannot expect reporters, columnists, and reviewers to come knocking on my door unless I send them a news release telling them that I have done something newsworthy.

As with my other file categories, I started with a list of local media contacts. I filed the names of the editors of the school newspaper, school parent-teacher newsletter, and church bulletin. Moving a bit farther afield, I included the names of local newspaper editors, who are in the business of featuring residents in their distribution areas. Since these contacts can change, it is a good idea to check them before sending every news release. To be prepared to distribute your news of fast-breaking developments to local newspapers and radio and television stations, call for and file their fax numbers (or e-mail addresses) ahead of time.

Reporters all over the world cover the entertainment beat. It is never too early to start filling your media contact file with editors and columnists of show business trade papers, reviewers, radio hosts, and television commentators. After receiving your mailings through the years, your name will ring a bell when you do something outstanding.

Finally, begin filing the names of publicists you hope to hire in the future. You can check the Yellow Pages for advertising and consulting firms that handle public relations. Publicists also are mentioned in articles about celebrities. That is how I learned Annette Wolf handles publicity for Cindy Crawford, for example.

Remember family and friends

Relatives, teachers, former directors, and other friends enjoy following my career. With their names on file, I remember to send them news releases, postcards, and newsletters. Besides, you never know. Someone who knows someone may know someone....

As careers progress, databases can expand into more categories. You may need a broker to handle your stock transactions and a Realtor to find you a home with a pool. It is always useful to record recommendations for voice, dance, and acting coaches, hairdressers, makeup artists, photographers, personal trainers, dentists, and medical specialists. Ultimately, you can aspire to know and be known by all the producers, directors, playwrights, and screenwriters your database might include.

How to reach your market by mail

Writing to your file names would be easier if you knew more about the people behind them. Be alert to ways to find as much information as possible about the individuals and organizations listed in your database. Learn about agents and managers by asking for referrals the way you ask other students what they know about a teacher you will have next semester. Before requesting that a local community theatre consider you for an internship or for future roles, attend plays there. Be prepared to make informed comments about what attracted you to the theatre's productions.

Information can come to you from all sorts of sources—you just have to pay attention. You may see an agent mentioned in an article about an actor, read what a manager said when she appeared on a panel discussion, listen to a story an actor tells during an interview, and keep track of the topics that interest a reporter. Add facts such as these to the names in your database. Drawing on this kind of information will enable you to include a personalized note with your mailings.

Saying something specific is always more effective than gushing about how you have loved "the theatre" all your life and would do anything to get into show business. If you know nothing about the people named in your file, your cover letter or postcard message can say something specific about you. What you get across can begin with the color of the envelope you use (I use blue) and conclude with an interesting P.S. to your cover letter.

Call attention to a role you have played, to callbacks you have had for professional parts, to your training with a well-known acting coach. Messages on the picture postcards you send to follow up a picture/resume mailing should always focus on career progress and up-to-the-minute news, reporting, for example, that you have just been accepted in a competitive theatre program or cast in an upcoming production.

Mailings have to continue throughout an actor's career. Just as you are trying to find out more about the people in your files, they will be finding out more about you. It may take years before they begin to recognize your face and name, get a feel for your performing strengths, and respond. Like any advertising campaign for a brand-name product, your headshots, postcards, newsletters, promotional fliers for plays, news releases, and media kits are designed to create and reinforce your image—the first step to a sale.

You can simplify this mailing process by buying preprinted, peel-off labels with names of agents, casting directors, producers, and others from companies such as the Shakespeare Theatrical Mailing Service listed in Appendix B. You also can create a more personal list by adding extra names to the Shakespeare database and/or by requesting labels for specific segments—for example, agents who specialize in young people or in commercials, film, soaps, television, or industrials.

The importance of reminding the show business world that you are a working part of it cannot be ignored. If you are too busy to develop and maintain your own database and to write individual cover letters, use computer-generated labels and letters. Customized letters are far better, however. The personal touch is always preferable. Not surprisingly, direct mail research indicates that hand-addressed letters are more effective than labels—especially those applied haphazardly. And a letter or postcard sent to an individual agent within an agency carries more weight than material sent just to the agency in general.

Finally, there is the constant problem of updating personnel and addresses and deleting businesses that leave the field. Whether maintaining your own files or relying on a label supplier, how old a list is determines how effective it is. I usually request a new SAG list from the Philadelphia office every six months. No matter how perfect your message, sending it to the wrong person can be worthless.

Publicity news releases
and media kits set you apart

How often have we all heard that we are in a very competitive field where luck and contacts can be more important than talent? Publicity offers a way to improve your odds of being discovered and to increase the number of people who know you. There is a scene in the movie *Easter Parade* when Fred Astaire tells Judy Garland that she is not a woman who turns heads. Walking ahead of him, she makes a strange face. Suddenly, passersby cannot take their eyes off of her. Being offbeat, beautiful, talented, or funny is not enough. Someone has to take notice. That is the aim of publicity—to make as many people as possible take notice.

Just as agents and casting directors are used to looking at headshots when they make decisions about whom to bring in for an audition, editors often rely on news releases to help them decide which stories to cover. A news release consolidates vital information, usually on one page. It requires an attention-getting headline. The opening paragraph should include all the newsworthy who, what, where, why, and how facts. For local media, try to mention connections to the geographic area which those publications or TV and radio stations cover. When Mom wrote the news release about my job at the Philadelphia Phillies, she improved my newsworthiness in the eyes of neighborhood newspapers by saying that I attended a local high school (see news release example, Fig. 7, page 39).

News releases often include a quote the media can use, and they always provide some background material. Reporters expect a news release to include a telephone number and a contact person, other than yourself, that they can call for additional information. You could use a parent's name and home telephone number, but you also could make up a name, ask your grandmother to handle calls, use an answering service, or develop some other creative means to respond to queries inspired by your news release.

For a special event, such as a movie premiere, publicists go all out to generate publicity by preparing media kits that may include a number of news releases along with other items. When young actors help a church put on a talent show, publish a play, conduct a survey, or provide leadership for any special project, they also need to distribute media kits designed to generate articles and broadcast coverage. You can make your own kit by filling a two-pocket folder with news releases about your accomplishment, a picture/resume, a newsletter, business card, a fact sheet telling where you were born, something about your family, your academic record and awards, and any other human-interest information from your background.

If the news release and/or media kit works and you are featured in a television segment, radio interview, magazine column, or newspaper article, such as the one on my baseball job (Fig. 8, page 40), maximize your exposure. Send copies of the segment or the article to agents, casting directors, managers and others whom you are trying to impress. You also can include these new publicity items in your next media kit. In short, recycle your good publicity the same way movies and plays do when they fill their advertisements with favorable quotes written by reviewers.

Young actors need to get in the habit of making themselves newsworthy. Celebrities work on political campaigns, raise money for charities, coach Little League teams, take up causes, testify at hearings, participate in sporting events, appear on talk shows. Is there any opportunity for you in these areas? Keep your eyes open for the names of organizers you should contact in order to get involved. Look them up in your telephone book or go to the library to look up their addresses and numbers in out-of-town directories. Send letters or call to express your interest and to ask or suggest what you can do. Once you are involved in a newsworthy event, send news releases, a publicity photo and/or a media kit to your publicity contacts. Actors need to contact everyone with a project to cast. Publicity helps us make our rounds.

Fig. 7: A news release

NEWS RELEASE

Contact: LuAnne Feik -- (610) xxx-xxxx
FOR IMMEDIATE RELEASE

TAKE ME OUT TO THE BALL GAME

WEST CHESTER, May 3, 1997 — Annie Jay, a senior at Great Valley High School, has the perfect summer job. She is one of 16 "Phanstormers" the Philadelphia Phillies hired to entertain baseball fans before home games and between innings.

"We play trivia games, do skits, get fans to perform, and give away prizes," said Jay.

This fall, Jay will attend the American Academy of Dramatic Arts in New York City. She has appeared locally in "The Tempest" at the West Chester and Barleysheaf Playhouse and in "A Christmas Carol" at Hedgerow Theatre.

###

(Note: Those three little #'s tell the editor that this is the end of the release; if there were a second page, it would say "more".)

Fig. 8: This is the article that ran in the paper, as a result of our news release.

DAILY LOCAL NEWS

SPORTS

Section

C

Sunday, July 13, 1997

Leading the Phillies' fans

Staff photo by Amy Dragoo

Recent Great Valley High School graduate Annie Jay does her best to entertain fans during Philadelphia Phillies baseball games at Veterans Stadium.

Showing 'em a good time

By TERRI CO. K
Staff Writer

The Phillies have been painful to watch lately, having so far recorded the worst record in the major leagues. Between the poor pitching outings and on-field errors, someone must entertain the fans who still visit Veterans Stadium.

Annie Jay, a recent Great Valley High School graduate, is among those who ensure that the fans who venture to the Vet go home happy regardless of what the Phillies do on the field.

Jay and her fellow "Phanstormers" roam the stadium to entertain fans before the game and between innings. They ask trivia questions, tell jokes, perform skits and give out prizes.

"The goal of the Phillies organization is the fans," Jay said. She is one of 16 performers who give suffering Phillies fans a reason to smile.

"When we're really necessary is when the other team scores nine runs in the third inning," she said.

Jay stumbled into the summer job at an audition for the East Coast Theater Conference. A scout there asked her to try out for the Phillies. So, she showed her improvisational skills to the Phillies' director of marketing.

"They just wanted to see that I had a lot of energy," Jay said.

The actress has some local theatre experience. She performed in "The Tempest" for the West Chester and Barley Sheaf Players, and in "A Christmas Carol" at Hedgerow Theatre.

But for her summer job, she has no script on which to fall back. "The first couple games, I was a little nervous," she admitted. "But the fans really respond well."

One Phanstormer activity involves playing "Where's Waldo" with a section of spectators. A fan must pick the performer out of the crowd in order to win a T-shirt.

Jay, the youngest of the Phanstormers, had only a few practices before the home opener. "We're really encouraged to make up new things every day," she said.

"Something interesting usually happens at every game because we talk to so many people," Jay said.

Although she has always been a big baseball fan, Jay said, "I hadn't been that into the Phillies, but I've gotten to be a big Phillies fan."

She will miss the end of the season when she leaves for college in New York in the fall. The actress will attend the American Academy of Dramatic Arts.

Jay said she expects her Phillies experience will help her with her future career.

"It's definitely given me a lot of confidence with large groups of people," she said.

Chapter 4: Next Steps

Entertainment Unions • Web Sites

One of the first questions I had for my manager was, "Should I join a union?" Nowadays, young actors are also asking, "Should I have a Web site?" In the long run the answer to both questions is probably, "Yes." In the short run, the high costs of both options require a careful analysis of union benefits and an Internet presence.

Union membership represents professionalism

Professional actors who belong to enter- tainment unions cannot accept nonunion roles in the fields those unions represent. For a young actor, such a prohibition may prove to be a serious limitation. At the beginning of a career, gaining broad, frequent experience is more productive than constantly facing tough com- petition for union work.

Community theatre productions, dinner theatres, student films, and internships that are *not* covered by union contracts all help lengthen resumes. This is an important objective, because failure to get a part, or even an audition, is more often due to lack of ex- perience rather than lack of union membership. Even- tually, though, the more experience actors have, the more likely it is that they will be required to sign a union contract to work in a union-covered production some- where along the way. Union membership, after a certain point, can therefore be used as a leading indicator of what and how much an actor has done.

Union members can continue to look for their own jobs on a freelance basis without repre- sentation by agents, but if they have representation, they agree to use only union franchised agents. The relationship between a union member and a union franchised agent is governed by a contract, usually a one-year exclusive representation agreement. Under union rules, an actor can terminate this agreement after a given period by explaining specifics in a letter to the agent and the union.

A union franchised agent operates much like an owner of a McDonald's franchise. In each case, the franchise holder agrees to abide by standards estab- lished by the parent organization. For example, union rules *prohibit* agents from instructing the actors they represent to go to a certain photographer and from re- questing fees for headshots, registration, or any service. Unions set agent commissions at ten percent and ensure that these commissions cannot reduce an actor's earnings from rehearsals, performances, and residuals below minimum scale. Union rules also require franchised agents to book union members only in productions covered by union contracts and to ask actors to perform in these productions only if they are offered and sign union-approved contracts.

Union jurisdiction is specific rather than generic. For example, a member of the Screen Actors Guild (SAG), represented by a SAG-franchised agent, can sign a contract to perform in a SAG-covered production. An actor who is a member of another entertainment union, such as Actors' Equity Association (AEA, or "Equity"), is required to join the Screen Actors Guild in order to work as a principal on a SAG project.

Each entertainment union has jurisdiction over different types of productions, but distinctions are not always clear-cut. It would be easy to say that the Screen Actors Guild covers all projects that are *filmed* and that the American Federation of Television and Radio Artists (AFTRA) has jurisdiction over programs that are *taped*. In fact, SAG membership may signify that an actor has been in filmed commercials, motion pictures, and/or industrials, but it also could mean that the performer has appeared in a music video, television series, sitcom, or other TV show which was taped at an independent studio, one not owned by a major network. (To further complicate matters, as we go to press, AFTRA and SAG are considering a merger.)

Actors are eligible to join the Screen Actors Guild when they sign contracts for principal or speaking roles in SAG-covered projects. Extras need to work three days on a SAG production before they are eligible for membership. SAG also considers actors eligible for membership if they have been members of AEA, or of AFTRA, for one year and can prove that they have had principal or speaking roles. SAG has a sizeable initiation fee ($1,152 at present) and basic annual dues ($85). As earnings under SAG contracts go up, annual dues increase as well.

The American Federation of Television and Radio Artists covers members who work in radio, live television, and *videotaped* network and local television shows, commercials, and industrials. This includes announcers and disc jockeys as well as actors. In fact, all who want to join AFTRA can, as long as they pay an initiation fee and dues for six months. At the other extreme, actors can work on an AFTRA project without joining the union for up to thirty days. To continue beyond that period or to work on another AFTRA project, however, actors must pay the union's initiation fee ($1,000 as of this writing) and half of the basic annual fee ($85). Like SAG, AFTRA's annual dues go up as earnings under union contracts increase.

Actors' Equity Association membership is open to actors, chorus members, and stage managers who have worked in Broadway, off-Broadway, regional, dinner, and summer stock theatres covered by Equity contracts, as well as in Equity-covered touring companies and live industrials. Those producing projects under AEA jurisdiction are legally bound to hold separate auditions for union members and nonunion actors. Agents can submit appropriate nonunion actors for AEA auditions, and Equity producers can offer nonunion actors AEA contracts at any time. By signing these contracts and paying union dues, actors become Equity performers.

Nonunion actors also have other ways to become AEA members. Equity theatres may offer Membership Candidate programs that enable nonunion actors to progress toward AEA membership by performing for 50 weeks in roles covered by the "non-pro" (i.e., nonprofessional) ratios in Equity theatre contracts. A Membership Candidate can cut the required time in a nonunion role to 40 weeks by passing a test on Actors' Equity Association rules. Equity membership is also open to those who are members of SAG, AFTRA, and other entertainment unions, if they meet two conditions: they have been union members for one year, and they have been under union jurisdiction once as a principal or "under-five" (a speaking role with fewer than five lines), or for three days as an extra. Equity has an initiation fee ($800 as of this writing) and collects basic biannual dues (equal to $156 per year right now) or a percentage of earnings, whichever is greater. Payments can be spread out and deducted from AEA paychecks for a year or longer.

In addition to the three unions mentioned, some others that entertainers join are listed in Appendix B. The American Guild of Musical Artists (AGMA), for example, covers solo artists (singers, dancers, instrumentalists), chorus members, choreographers, and stage directors and managers involved with opera, concert, recital, and ballet performances. Singers, dancers, and comedians who perform in musical revues may join the American Guild of Variety Artists (AGVA). At any time, an actor can send a self-addressed, stamped business envelope to a union's local or the national office to request membership information and an application form. Initiation fees for actors who join a second and third union are reduced. In all cases, actors can deduct their union dues as business expenses on their income tax forms.

Entertainment unions require members to use professional names that are not identical or similar to those of other union members. If their names are already "taken," new union members will be informed that they will have to alter their names or take new "stage" names. Just as a registerred trademark protects the manufacturer that incurred the cost and effort of developing a brand name, the union name requirement prevents one actor from trading on the hard-won reputation built by another.

What do these unions do for actors in exchange for the fees and dues they collect? Local union offices may operate telephone hotlines that alert members to projects being cast in the area. To protect members, unions also establish working condition guidelines. Rules require performers under 18 to be given time for school and rest. They can require the presence of a parent and nurse and stipulate when a child's work day has to end. An AFTRA-SAG collaboration produced the *Young Performers Handbook*, which is available to both union and nonunion actors. You can request a copy by writing to any of the AFTRA or SAG offices listed in Appendix B.

Producers agree to pay salary scales offered in union contracts. A theatre's pre-tax box office receipts over the last three years, for example, are used to determine a stage actor's minimum weekly salary scale. Payment for doing a commercial depends on the size of the markets where it is shown. Union contracts establish not only pay scales but also health insurance benefits and pension plans. Ongoing efforts to merge SAG and AFTRA may combine their retirement plans in the future. SAG, AFTRA, and AEA already have cooperated to form the Actors Federal Credit Union (AFCU), a tax-exempt banking service that provides free checking, dividends on savings accounts, and low-interest loans exclusively to union and association members in the performing arts.

A Web site could help you click

Young actors and the World Wide Web are growing up together. On campuses, where e-mail and online research are a way of life, student activity committees already check Web sites to find the comedians, musical groups, and other entertainers they book for college gigs.

In traditional theatrical, film, and television circles, however, casting by computer remains in its infancy. At the moment, the relatively small number of actors posted on many scattered Web sites discourages directors from using these casting resources. For a fee, some Web sites offer to post actors' headshots and resumes the way a directory—such as the *Players' Guide*—publishes them. In fact, as of 1998, the $100 entry fee union members paid to be listed in the *Players' Guide* directory also covered a listing in CD-ROM format and on the Internet. Most casting Web sites charge an additional fee every time an actor updates online resume information.

Before signing up for any casting Web site, bear in mind the limited extent, currently, of online casting. Investigate a specific Web site by trying various keywords to see how easy it would be for anyone, especially a casting director, to find the Web site. Check out the way headshots and resumes look online, and find out how many actors appear. From the perspective of a casting director, an electronic agency should offer thousands of choices. CastNet (www.castnet.com) claims to have 35,000 actor clients, acquired by allowing agents to post their client rosters free of charge, and by signing up an additional 10,000 actors without representation, who pay $150 for a basic listing (more for video and audio). However, the jury is still out on to what extent casting directors actually use the Web site.

At present, most casting directors continue to rely on agents who satisfy their requests by looking through headshots and picture postcards in metal filing cabinets, not in computerized databases. To get into those metal files, actors must continue to use "snail mail" to submit their picture/resumes.

Nonetheless, casting by computer bears watching, because it probably will play a much larger role in our acting futures. There are at least two potential directions for growth: an expansion of sites actors can scan for employment and more actors on sites which casting directors can scan.

Theatres now using Web sites to sell season ticket packages might as easily use them to post casting notices. Young actors can get an idea of the casting information already available on the Net by visiting several sites. *Back Stage*, one of the periodicals in Appendix B, maintains a Web site, www.backstage.com, that posts casting notices online before they are published. All online articles and a partial casting list are free. The monthly subscription fee for full audition listings is $9.95. Performers can speed their online search at this site by designating job type, such as non-Equity stage or student film, and location—West Coast, Los Angeles, Chicago, Florida, East Coast, New York City. At another site, you can sample the auditions and grant offerings on www.rtuh.com/adl before deciding if you want to pay $12 a year for access to a complete listing.

If you want to limit your search to Manhattan and Los Angeles, and search for opportunities based on your gender, age, film, stage, or other specifics, check www.buzz.com. You have to register with name, password, and e-mail designation, but the service is free. At www.playbill.com, all types of performers and technical personnel will find openings, mainly in Equity theatres, throughout the United States. Dates show when the notices were first posted. At www.actorsequity.org, union and "non-required," or nonunion, principals and chorus members can tap into audition notices provided by AEA offices in New York, Chicago, Los Angeles, Orlando, and San Francisco. The Internet also hosts newsgroups for those who want to discuss various aspects of the theatre. Key in rec.arts.theatre, and, depending on your interest, add .plays, .musicals, .stagecraft, or .misc.

In addition to using virtual casting sites as a means to find auditions, young actors who have grown up as Internet users cannot help but think about creating Web sites to promote their careers. The challenge is to create an interactive site that people want to visit.

Off-the-shelf software that essentially pastes a headshot, resume and news release to an electronic billboard will not stop millions of browsers or merit must-see bookmarking. Yet, seeking assistance from an ad agency or other professional Web site designer is very expensive. Then, there are the costs of a host server, registering a domain name, listing a Web site on major search engines, and updating information. I have seen price quotes for getting an elaborate corporate Web site up and running that range anywhere from $30,000 to $300,000!

Despite the high price tag, young actors should keep the idea of a personal Web site in the back of their minds. An opportunity to promote yourself to as many as 300 million by the year 2000 cannot be dismissed. Actors known to attract attention on the Net show agents and producers that they have a virtual following ready to buy real tickets.

What might unknown performers do to draw an audience to their Web sites? They could provide their up-to-the-minute personal takes on current films, fads, TV shows, books, and other events. Actors could let their fans hear a voice clip, while they respond to questions, or they could ask their audiences to react to a joke they wrote or graphics and video showing them with short red or long black hair. They could come up with other interactive devices: a question of the day, a contest for a new award show, classic film trivia, and case studies of how to land an amateur or professional part. Of course, actors would have to be careful not to provide any information someone could use to stalk them.

To promote their Web sites, actors would include their Internet addresses on all headshots, resumes, picture postcards, business cards, newsletters, and news releases. With luck, reporters might include a Web address in feature articles and television segments on an actor. Generating an Internet buzz may eventually become one of the best things new actors can do to make agents, casting directors, and producers notice them.

Today's talented amateur can visualize a professional acting future that includes membership in one or more entertainment unions, signing with union-franchised agents, surfing the Net for job opportunities, and constantly updating a personal Web site that millions want to see. For the moment, however, the best thing most young actors can do is: find opporutnities to perform.

Chapter 5: And the Winner Is...

Promotional Contests • Beauty Pageants and Model Searches • Rewards and Drawbacks

According to some estimates, agents fill 75 percent of all professional acting jobs. Young actors without agents must find their own opportunities. In a newspaper or on television, they, their parents, teachers or friends are sure to see an announcement offering the chance to be the next Miss Texas or Oscar Mayer kid. For a beauty pageant or promotional talent search, organizers need maximum publicity to make their event a success. The more competitors who try out to be the new Annie, Mikey, or Little Miss Hawaiian Tropic, the more likely the spectacle will be covered on the evening news. Every contestant trying to rise to the top in this kind of hurlyburly audition atmosphere helps an event organizer look good. For a few lucky winners, these events also can be the start of something big.

Thousands flock to contests

You can expect newspaper ads and TV spots to attract thousands of competitors. Before September's "Miss America" contest in Atlantic City, thousands of women compete in state pageants around the country. For an opportunity to model back-to-school fashions, young people flock to department stores to try their luck walking down a runway. The taller ones have a chance to model; the others decide they might as well console themselves with some shopping.

TV shows and commercials make news when they come to town to cast a part. A television station in Philadelphia went after ratings by promising to select one child from the first 1,000 snapshots submitted by parents who wanted their preschoolers to be on Bill Cosby's show. Life cereal looked at 35,000 boys and girls before deciding Marli Brianna Hughes would be the new Mikey. Likewise, Oscar Mayer's ten Wienermobiles might search for TV stars in as many as 100 towns during a summer season. At each location, reporters come out to see 150 youngsters, 3 to 12 years old, sing the "Oscar Mayer Wiener Jingle" or the "Bologna Song." Many compete, but only the best performer wins a $20,000 college scholarship and appears in an Oscar Mayer commercial.

Beauties and models smile and strut their stuff

Some beauty pageants also offer opportunities to win scholarships and TV commercial contracts. Agents and managers often serve as judges and attend pageants to discover new talent. From babies to grandparents, actors who thrive on the pageant circuit can use these showcases to attract attention throughout their careers. Besides the televised "Miss Teen USA," "Miss America," "Miss USA," and "Miss Universe" contests, there are thousands of other competitions to keep beauties and their families busy every weekend in the year.

Unfortunately, I am not a beauty pageant person. My experience began and ended with a fifth-place finish in Pennsylvania's Junior Star Pageant. In the summer after I turned eight, my mother and I bought my long competition dress at a bridal discount store and headed for Harrisburg. I already had white shoes, tights, and the blue shorts the contest required.

Contest participation costs easily escalate. Besides the price of clothes, travel, and an overnight hotel stay, I could have used some runway training at a modeling school. You should not have to pay a fee to learn a pageant's rules, who the judges are, and what your prizes and obligations will be if you win. There are entry fees, however, sometimes separate ones for best eyes, smile, talent, and other categories. In my case, contestants were expected to sell at least one page of ads for a program book. Entrance instructions explained how I should ask retailers and clubs to sponsor me. Thanks to an ad my aunt purchased for her business, I had the minimum financial support I needed to enter the contest.

Arriving for the pageant, Mom and I noticed the other contestants had enormous dresses. Billows of tulle covered half of the chairs in the meeting room. The pageant coordinator told us the competition would develop our self-confidence and promote friendships. She stressed that this contest was more appropriate for our age group than others in which girls wore makeup and adult fashions.

Along with poise and friendships, the beauty contest payoff can come in the form of cash, bonds, cars, scholarships, vacations, modeling contracts, commercials, and TV and film roles. It also can come in the form of a year's supply of something you will never use. At the end of my Junior Star Pageant orientation meeting on Friday evening, all of us were invited to come forward for gifts. This is when I knew my temperament was unsuited for beauty pageants. The 1986 Miss Pennsylvania Junior Star was first in line. She was given a Strawberry Shortcake book that I could have read when I was four. Just about jumping with glee, this ten-year-old threw her arms around the pageant coordinator's neck as though she had just won a pony. I took my book and walked away in disgust.

The next morning's interview portion of the competition was more to my liking. With each judge, I enjoyed a pleasant conversation, not only about where I went to school and what subjects I liked but also about what I wanted to be and the issues of the day. By the time we reached the pageant's final questioning phase, I announced that I wanted to find a cure for AIDS. Others were content to say that they hoped to be models and moms.

Part of our pageant weekend was devoted to practicing a dance routine and walking down the run-way we would use for Sunday's evening-gown judging. During these preparations, one of the assistants said that she liked my coloring. The coordinator told her she should consider instead who *best supported* the contest. Perhaps this was the deciding factor. The girl who eventually became 1987's Miss Pennsylvania Junior Star sold at least eight pages of ads in the program book.

With the pageant finale at hand, it was time to put on our long dresses. I brushed my hair while hot rollers, curling irons, and hair spray sizzled around me. Helped by their mothers, my competitors stacked on frilly petticoats. Ruffled and beribboned blue, pink, white, and yellow dresses gently floated down over their heads to create a room full of little Scarlett O Hara's. Wearing a dress with a white eyelet top and rose taffeta skirt unsupported by crinolines, I looked limp by comparison.

In about a minute I was zipped and seated with Mom in the waiting area, watching the others still primping. The mother of the 1986 winner joined us. Gesturing toward a little blonde, she asked, "Do you know why that girl's mom told her not to jump around?" She's wearing a false hairpiece," she said, answering her own question.

Between the parade of contestants and the tally of judges' votes, the M.C. had time to kill. He asked, "Does anyone here want to break dance?" My brother had just taught me some moves, and I raised my hand to volunteer. The M.C. looked at me in my long dress spinning around on the floor and said that he had never seen anyone in a beauty contest respond that way. Like I said, I am not pageant material.

Young women who are attuned to the beauty pageant process begin their climb toward "Miss Teen USA" at the state level. In my state of Pennsylvania, each contestant is asked to raise a sponsorship fee of more than $600 to cover expenses for the three-day competition, awards, pageant-show production costs, and the state winner's trip to the national finals. Applicants have to be least 15 and under 19 years old on July 1 and at least a six-month resident of the state. They have to certify that they have never been married and that they are neither pregnant nor a mother. Young women are judged in swimsuits, evening gowns, and personality interviews. Unlike the "Miss America" pageant, there is no performing talent competition, and one-piece swimsuits are required. A personal history form asks contestants, among other things, to list their favorite foods and three words that describe them.

Beauty Pageants and
Model Searches: Rewards and Drawbacks

Beauty pageant and model search winners can make contacts that launch lifelong careers. Charlotte Lopez was living in foster care, as she had all her life, when she saw a newspaper ad for the "Miss Vermont Teen USA" pageant. Going business to business, person to person, she raised the $595 entrance fee and won. Not only that, she went on to become the 1993 "Miss Teen USA," to sign with the William Morris Agency, and to begin her acting career in Los Angeles—where the convertible that had been part of her winnings proved most useful. "Junior Miss" competitions were just the beginning for national winner Diane Sawyer of *20/20* and Maryland's winner Kathie Lee Gifford. Back in 1971,

Oprah Winfrey was crowned "Miss Black Tennesssee." Tiffani-Amber Thiessen was 1988's "Miss Jr. America, Preteen" before she joined the cast of *Saved by the Bell!* and later *Beverly Hills 90210.* Cybill Shepherd got her start as the victor in a 1968 "Model of the Year" contest.

Before making a transition to an acting career, reed-thin, 5'7"-and-over beauty pageant winners often pursue modeling careers. For them, Michael Gross's book, *Model: The Ugly Business of Beautiful Women,* is a must-read. It warns of the destructive downside: too much money and freedom, dirty old men, alcohol, drugs, and backstabbing. It also shows how models like Cindy Crawford, who once won a "Look of the Year" competition sponsored by the Elite modeling agency, parlay their images into multimillion-dollar empires.

Chapter 6: Scams

Phony Agencies • Fees • Nudity • Official Help

Avoid phony casting agencies

Ads like this are tempting. Mom and I once responded to an advertisement for a free informational "seminar" sponsored by a company that claimed to be in the business of providing film extras. Along with about 200 others, we went to a local hotel conference room to hear the company's pitch.

A "casting" process such as the one we experienced should immediately raise some suspicions. Everyone was asked to complete a questionnaire and to get in line for an evaluation. We were told that we could come forward individually or, if we had come with friends, in groups. Those *not* invited to the next screening level at a New Jersey office building included not only a matron whose hair could have inspired Dennis Rodman, but also an attractive young woman who had a professional headshot.

At the time, we missed the warning signs. Mom and I kept my appointment in New Jersey the next day. What we found was a reception room decorated with headshots and composites taped to the wall. Handout copies of an article told how a client almost had been hired for a film. While a stereo blasted, I tried to memorize commercial sides for a strawberry-scented shampoo.

When I was called to deliver my lines on camera, I stumbled over one sentence. Not to worry. Mom and I were sent into a room to meet with "an agent." He had an English accent and claimed to have moved to New Jersey to avoid New York's hustle and bustle. To my mother's credit, she doubted that someone who *left* Manhattan's deal-making center knew what he was doing. Although my appointment at the casting company's office was less than twenty-four hours after the hotel "seminar," the agent told me that I was too late to be hired as an extra in the films mentioned only a day earlier. What he needed in order to represent me in the future was pictures. Could he schedule me for a sitting on Monday?

The price for a headshot was $500. A composite of four photos was $900. He needed an immediate, non-refundable check for half the amount in order to guarantee I would keep my appointment. He told me they had to pay the photographer, even when actors failed to honor their sitting times. They had just had a "Black Monday," he said, in his suave British accent, when three people had not kept their appointments. We did not have $450, or even $250, and we left. While we were waiting for the elevator, the agent appeared. He went to the water fountain and seemed to be listening to our conversation.

Was he curious to find out if we were thinking about reporting his operation to authorities? Apparently, some who signed up for photo sessions did just that. On a local television news program only a few months later, Mom and I saw the casting company's New Jersey office, completely empty. The photos taped to the wall had been easy to remove. The blaring stereo, screen-test camera, and agent, British accent and all, had vanished. The television reporter suggested consumers should not pay an agent for headshots and should check what information the Better Business Bureau has about show business recruiters.

This is also good advice for young actors who are asked to attend a school when they respond to an ad offering work. It often turns out that even after taking an endless array of makeup, hair, poise, and other courses, that first job always seems to be just one more class away. Schools, like every other firm the Better Business Bureau investigates, will have a Satisfactory or Unsatisfactory grade or a notation if for some reason no rating could be given.

Do I need to pay a fee?

Wise young actors know they will face unfamiliar practices when starting out in a new field. To avoid going to the Better Business Bureau when each new situation arises, find a drama teacher, school musical director, or, better yet, a trusted entertainment attorney to provide informed counsel. Getting in the habit of reading show business publications regularly also helps avoid mistakes.

When you understand how reputable agents, personal managers, and casting directors operate, you will know that they can make decisions based on the snapshots and picture/resume you send them. You do not have to pay hundreds of dollars to attend a convention where you probably will not find anyone to represent you. You will not have to pay to have your photo placed in a book that someone else sends to casting directors, and you will know that agents and managers do not charge you consultation, registration, or any other fees.

Some personal managers do charge for seminars that brief parents and young performers on how show business works. The information is valuable, but check around. Other managers, personal and business, may be offering similar sessions for free. Agencies franchised by the entertainment unions abide by rules prohibiting any charges for lessons, public relations, or photos. You should be free to choose your own photographer. Agents may recommend several photographers, but they cannot require you to use any of them, nor can they receive any monetary benefit from a referral. Most importantly, you owe nothing to an agent or manager until *after* you have worked.

What is definitely free is an audition. Yet actors have been asked to pay to join phony unions and membership organizations before even being considered for a role. Once you know how much a union's initiation fee is, however, you are not likely to send someone $250 for a phony union card. After I was chosen to perform in a children's theatre and a community playhouse, I did pay small fees, less than $50, to help cover production expenses. Obviously, I could have chosen not to accept the parts I won in open auditions. I figured it was my choice to pay for these experiences the same way I would pay for voice, tap, or acting lessons. The key fact is, it was a choice I was free to make after the audition.

On the fine day when you are hired to perform for pay, other questions arise. If you have a manager, the employer will send your paycheck to him. Managers will take out up to 25 percent in commissions before issuing a check for your share. Unscrupulous agents have been known to give actors ten percent commissions and pocket the actors' 90 percent for themselves. Union contracts govern how much and how soon you are paid, but there are no standard guidelines for nonunion work. Putting the amount due you and the timing for payment in writing before you begin a job can help avoid future disputes.

Beware the casting couch

The young actor needs to stay away from the proverbial casting couch. Unless you are a young man trying out for a part on a soap, keep your shirt on and do not be pressured to do any nude photo layouts or scenes. Any suggestion to meet after normal business hours in a private location should be viewed with suspicion. A scene in one of my favorite show business movies, "All that Jazz," shows a young dancer telling Bob Fosse how much she wants to be in films. He clearly indicates how much he wants her for something else, but she is too blinded by her ambition to get the message.

The fact is, nude photos last forever. If you do not want someone to see them now *or* in the future, do not agree to have any taken for any reason whatsoever. Remind yourself about what happened to Vanessa Williams. After she had already been named "Miss America," she had to give up her crown when suggestive photos from her past surfaced. No matter how much someone flatters you and claims shots will be tasteful, beautiful, and fun, walk away from the project, at least until you are comfortable with full exposure. Do not be tempted by ads offering $500 a week for dancers at stag parties or models who will become Internet stars. Audition notices for legitimate productions will mention which parts call for full or partial nudity, and contracts can spell out how nude scenes will be handled. Clearly, nudity can be relevant to a story. If you do not want to be the one to tell it, the challenge is having the courage to say "No."

Legal problems require remedies

Lawsuits to restrain magazines from publishing nude photos are not the only stories that highlight show business problems. We hear about parents who use up every cent a child star makes, or, in the case of Macaulay Culkin, grapple over who will manage and benefit from his career. Joanna Pacitti wins Macy's "Broadway's New Annie" contest and then never gets to play Annie on Broadway. A court tries to decide who wrote *Rent*. Movie stars due a percentage of profits can find themselves at the mercy of accounting practices that allow film companies to avoid showing a profit. Once they make money—even if they have made millions—actors can learn that they are in trouble with the IRS, because they or their business managers have failed to pay enough income taxes. After achieving success, actors also have found personal managers suddenly appearing to claim commissions they never earned, and screenwriters might hear out of the blue from authors who claim their work has been plagiarized.

An actor's joy in landing a part can easily turn to frustration. Overseas, producers have gone bankrupt and left performers stranded in a foreign country. Be sure you have a round trip ticket before leaving home. In *The Glam Scam*, listed in Appendix B, author Erik Joseph reminds actors to never give anyone their passports when they are performing abroad. A passport is your ticket in and out of a foreign country. While working outside the U.S., you are subject to foreign laws requiring green cards for aliens and proper visas. Find out what your host country requires by contacting its embassy in Washington, D.C., and be sure you know the location and telephone number of the U.S. embassy at your destination. And, of course, do not sign an overseas employment contract written in a foreign language you do not understand.

Performers need contracts, or just a letter signed by both parties, to protect them at home as well. Summer stock interns, for example, may realize too late that they should have asked more questions about the length of their workdays, their salary, when it is paid, their living conditions, who pays for housing, meals, and transportation, and what opportunities they will have to perform. Taking tickets, making costumes, painting scenery, and parking cars are legitimate activities for young actors in stock, but will they also have a chance to audition for parts?

Actors need to keep good records of correspondence, contracts, checks, and promotional materials in case it becomes necessary to make a case. A wide variety of government and private agencies stand ready to right injustices. To start the ball rolling, call local consumer affairs and human rights departments, the small claims court, the police department's frauds division, the regional office of the Federal Trade Commission, and the mail-fraud section of the local U.S. Postal Service. *The Glam Scam* provides a useful state-by-state guide to laws affecting actors and models, as well as a listing of government offices that may be able to help. Investigative and consumer advocate reporters can be allies, as can the Volunteer Lawyers for the Arts, the Casting Society of America, and the entertainment unions listed in Appendix B.

The best defense is caution. Remember that no unions establish rules for personal managers, modeling, or print work. You can bring problems with business managers who are certified public accountants or attorneys to the professional accounting societies or bar associations that set standards for these professions, but using any professional, governmental, or legal process to resolve a dispute will be time-consuming and possibly costly. Ads for fresh faces and new talent are suspect. Remember, too, that established agents, personal managers, and business managers do not need to advertise in a newspaper or on television in the first place. They already know of more talent than they can possibly represent.

Chapter 7: The Moment of Truth

Auditions • Combined Auditions • Monologues
Cold Readings • Improv • Callbacks

Legitimate show business opportunities can have an elaborate selection process—quite the opposite of the "no experience necessary" advertised by scam artists. Whether you are trying out for a role in the school musical, trying to impress an agent, or trying to become the new spokesperson for a leading brand of toothpaste, the crucial element is often the audition.

Early auditions are usually informal and easy. Thinking back to fifth grade, I cannot remember any tension connected with my first attempt to land a part in *Joseph and the Amazing Technicolor Dreamcoat.* Our school's musical director played a song two times. It was new to me, but ten days after I sang it for the first time, I was chosen as the play's narrator.

For future school musicals, my preparations were a little more extensive. Public Television conveniently aired a British version of *Oliver!* just before I tried out for the part of The Artful Dodger. Before we did *Bye Bye Birdie,* I had an opportunity to see Tommy Tune's revival. From the moment I saw an *Annie* video, I knew I wanted the part of Miss Hannigan. Prior to my auditions for these shows, I not only watched other productions but I also practiced singing and dancing to tapes in front of a mirror in the garage.

In the big time, actors can find themselves in nerve-wracking situations where they have no way to prepare. For commercial and TV show auditions, I have left for Baltimore, Philadelphia, or New York early in the morning without knowing what lay in store. Even an agent or a manager often cannot brief an actor about the advertised product, a line's context in a script, or what the casting director wants except for age and gender.

Sometimes I had an appointment; other times, I attended an open call where anyone could be seen during a stated time period. At some point during the day, I would be called for what I have dubbed "a look and a line." Typically, I entered a room where there was a director, camera, monitor, and someone who operated the camera. The director would ask me to state my name, or "slate," and say my line. Once, there were no lines, and I was asked to improvise a bus stop conversation with another actor. The director did comment favorably that we were the first couple who faced the camera while performing our extemporaneous skit.

Auditions are perfect little performances

Auditions take various forms, but they have many similarities. By and large, they are the only way young actors will get a part, an agent, a manager, a scholarship, or even get into a college drama program.

All headshots, mailings, and training are a waste of money unless an actor is willing to face that moment of truth, the audition, over and over again. Before going to an audition, I almost always remind myself of the 12 guideposts that Michael Shurtleff describes in *Audition*, a book you'll find listed in Appendix B. Open *Audition* to any page, and you will find an inspiring idea. Shurtleff reminds actors that we have to be heard, stand in the light to be seen, and always audition.

At auditions, some actors try to make themselves memorable by wearing a hat, glasses, a purple sweater, or scarf. Once, when a casting director asked us all to stand in a semicircle and say our names one after another in turn, I remember a girl singling herself out by dropping to her knees when she announced her identity. I was standing in the shadows over on the side when I said my name. I did not get a part. Auditioning for the same company the next year, I was closer to the middle, said my name clearly without histrionics, and was cast as a cat.

Auditions require a perfect performance before a very limited audience. No pressure there! I have read statements by casting directors who say an actor should view them as friends who want to be dazzled by your talent. In audition waiting rooms, I have seen signs proclaiming, "Relax, we think you're wonderful!" An article about auditions for Juilliard's freshman class quoted a drama professor telling students to imagine he was writing how great they were when they saw him making notes. But in large measure, whether an audition jury comes into a room as friends or foes is irrelevant. None of these "helpful hints" affects their predispositions. My job is to move them once they are there, to make them laugh or sigh in spite of themselves.

Just as actors cannot allow the attitudes of those viewing their auditions to affect them, they cannot be distracted by the setting where their auditions take place. At my first interview with a manager in her New York apartment, she gestured to me to sit next to her on a couch surrounded with clutter. The telephone rang incessantly. While talking to me, she and her assistant, who was barely visible behind stacks of papers and headshots on the dining room table, were making arrangements with parents to schedule auditions. The telephone continued to ring as I stood in front of a piano doing a monologue and singing without accompaniment. Pretending there were no distractions, I concentrated on my performance.

Combined auditions reach a wider audience

At combined auditions young actors have a chance to display their perfect little performances to representatives of as many as 90 theatre companies, theme parks, outdoor dramas, Shakespearean festivals, and other performance venues. In one weekend, usually in February or March, summer theatres and resident companies, as well as theatre schools and conservatories, look at hundreds of actors and technicians.

Each combined audition has its own deadline, registration fee, application procedure, and requirements for monologues, singing, and dancing. To obtain details, applicants can send self-addressed, stamped business-sized envelopes to the addresses in Appendix B. Some of the listed combined auditions, such as the New England Theatre Conference, require participants to be at least 18. Others are restricted to performers with a certain amount or type of experience. The League of Resident Theatres (LORT), for example, holds combined auditions open only to Equity members. Since hundreds of Equity professionals compete for LORT's slots, a lottery drawing selects which actors will actually be allowed to audition.

The application forms that I have received from the East Central Theatre Conference (ECTC) and the New England Theatre Conference (NETC) have requested information about my experience and a wallet-sized photo, not an 8"x10" headshot. Students, who pay a reduced fee, may be required to supply copies of student ID's and teacher recommendations. These applications also ask participants to send a stamped, self-addressed envelope that is used to return information about the day and time of an assigned audition and other more general instructions.

For some young actors, a combined audition may provide their first experience performing out of town. Thinking through what to bring and having everything ready before the last minute helps ease the tension. Remember headshots, because you will need them for callbacks. To help you locate the audition site (often a hotel), you will need a map of the area. You may need to find others to share the cost of the drive, a cab, and hotel room. When a snowstorm was forecast at the time of one of my combined auditions, Mom and I left a day early.

The first thing to do at a combined audition is check in at the registration desk. There you pick up a packet that contains, among other things, a conference schedule, diagram of room locations, and a list of theatres, productions, casting directors, conservatories, and other recruiters. A combined audition is divided into sessions. During each session, a number of actors are assigned to a warmup room and a room where they will perform one after another in front of those recruiters who choose to attend that session.

It is advisable to check into the warmup room anywhere from a half hour to an hour before your scheduled audition. Here, you will be told how to introduce yourself and your presentation, how you will be timed, and other important details. You will have a chance to vocalize and stretch, to go over your monologue, to make sure, if you are singing with taped accompaniment, that your tape is cued, and just to relax, knowing that you are in the right place on time and ready to go.

When I enter the audition room, I smile, give my introduction, and perform. As soon as "time" is called, I stop. It is very important not to plunge on or glare at the timekeeper. You may know that you timed your routine perfectly and that the audition clock is faulty, but you do not want to appear difficult and unwilling to take direction. Simply say, "Thank you," smile, and exit.

An hour or two after each audition session, callback sheets are posted on a main board. They tell which companies are interested in which actors. When I see my name on a callback sheet, I write down the name of the theatre, who wants to see me, and the casting director. Some theatre representatives want to meet you right away; others say they will call, or they ask you to leave your picture/resume somewhere.

If more than one theatre wants to see you at the same time, first try the one with fewer people waiting. Give all recruiters your complete attention. Even if you do not think that you want to work for a particular theatre, hear what its representative has to say. Given the volume of actors seen at combined auditions, it's best to send follow-up notes to the companies that you would like to perform with, expressing your interest in them.

The monologue treasure hunt

Actors may not be able to control the attitude of those who watch their auditions, their audition settings, or the weather, but generally they are told to choose their own audition monologue, song, or dance. Casting directors may ask to see a single five-minute monologue or two contrasting monologues of two minutes each, one contemporary and one classical. At some auditions, "classical" may be restricted to Shakespearean roles. When the audition is for a specific play or musical, notices may state whether or not you should prepare material from that work.

The problem is, there are not that many times in any play, especially modern ones, when an actor delivers a two- to five-minute uninterrupted speech. Besides, you want to audition with an age-appropriate part. Not only is the *Our Town* Stage Manager too old for any young actor, but his narrative explaining what is going on in Grover's Corners lacks dramatic impact. A monologue should have a kind of "to be or not to be" immediacy, where you demand someone understand or do something right now.

Actors looking for new monologues—or, for that matter, songs they can "sell"—will recognize such show-stoppers in a new play or recording. But what happens? Casting directors, agents, and college recruiters begin to hear the same audition material over and over again. You may even hear the person auditioning right before you doing "your" monologue or song.

I had my first experience delivering a prepared monologue when I auditioned for the High School for the Creative and Performing Arts in Philadelphia. At the library, using the keyword Monologues, I found collections for children, young actors, women, and men. Monologues also were grouped by contemporary, classical, and Renaissance periods. Usually a collection of monologues will give a little background for each monologue, including the name of the play from which it was taken, the author, age of the character, setting, mood, and a synopsis of the play.

After reading through several books, for my high school audition I chose the character Diana, in *Moving*, a 1991 comedy by Lee Kalcheim. Diana began her monologue by saying that she had gone to a Quaker school, but she did not fully agree with its noncompetitive philosophy. As an actor, I have to compete, and I had attended Friends Select, a wonderful Quaker school in Center City, Philadelphia. The role of Diana seemed like a good fit for me.

Years after I first did my Diana monologue, I tracked down a copy of *Moving*. When I read the entire play, I realized how lucky I had been that no one asked me questions about my character. In Act III, Diana tells us she is a lesbian, an aspect of the characterization which of course I had completely missed. I learned my lesson, and now read the entire play to understand my character completely, *before* learning a monologue. Finding new audition material is a lifelong quest. That one singular sensation—the well-suited monologue, song, or dance—changes with an actor's age, appearance, outlook, and experience.

Occasionally, materials received from a combined audition or college include monologue guidelines that read like instructions for heating a frozen pizza. They provide an insight into what those who came before you did wrong. Instead of saying, "Remove all packaging," there are directions telling you not to pour water on the stage and to avoid offensive language, stomach-turning descriptions, and overused material. Picture yourself as one of the summer theatre or college recruiters listening to hundreds of monologues. What would you like to see? A contemporary comedic piece done really well seems worth a try.

Besides selecting monologues from published collections, I have found it helpful to look beyond plays. The compelling material in *Letters of a Nation*, a reference listed in Appendix B, includes correspondence that outstanding Americans have written on the subjects of slavery, war, the death sentence, and being gay. Useful too are the early movies made by actors a young performer might resemble. If you consider yourself a young Audrey Hepburn, check out her *Sabrina*. The next Fred Astaire can study his moves in *You Were Never Lovelier* and *Blue Skies*. For those who look and sound like Jimmy Stewart, there is *Mr. Smith Goes to Washington*. Young women with attitude and an usual voice might recreate Tallulah Bankhead's early work in *Stage Door Canteen* or *Main Street to Broadway*. Classic films not only provide young actors with audition monologues, but they also serve as lessons in diction, phrasing, posture, movement, wardrobe, makeup, and hair styling. Several monologue collections and sources for classic plays and films are included in Appendix B.

Choosing the wrong monologue has dire consequences. Despite my name, I never dreamed of playing Annie. My favorite songs in the 1977 musical were "Little Girls" and "Easy Street." As Miss Hannigan in my final middle-school performance, I sang these songs to rousing ovations. Parents stood in the hall outside our dressing room chanting, "We love you, Miss Hannigan," when I emerged. The summer after this triumph, I had an audition with a management firm often credited with discovering Joey Lawrence. A manager took one look at my resume and reality crashed down around me, as he stated: "At age 14, you can't play Miss Hannigan." He was right.

I had a similar experience attempting my first Shakespearean monologue at a Renaissance Faire audition, when I was 15. There are relatively few Shakespearean monologues for women. I liked Desdemona's protestations in *Othello*. Again, I was told I was too young for the part. I chose a new monologue, Portia from *The Merchant of Venice*, and I finally landed my first Shakespearean role as the goddess Ceres and an understudy part as Ariel in *The Tempest* two years later. To gain admission to New York's American Academy of Dramatic Arts, I was prepared with my already proven and age-appropriate Diana from *Moving* and Ariel monologues. I also put these monologues on the demonstration tapes I used to apply for scholarships and admission to summer theatre programs.

Singers and dancers also need to prepare material for their auditions, as well as audio and videotapes. Contrasting ballad, up-tempo, or belt vocals or perhaps 16 bars of one song may be required. By searching through old music books and listening to classic albums, you can avoid choosing the same new songs that everyone else just "discovered."

When there is no accompanist, singers usually are expected to provide their music on audio tapes, not to sing *a capella*. If an accompanist is provided, singers need to bring sheet music that is written in the right key with the tempo clearly marked. Annie Lebeaux, musical director, vocal coach, and frequent audition accompanist, advises singers not to fold their sheet music in a way that can send it flying off the piano like a paper airplane. She suggests mounting a single piece of sheet music on cardboard. Multiple sheets should be printed on one side and mounted on cardboard accordion-style or placed in separate, non-glare plastic pockets in a ring binder.

At an audition, your first note has to be attacked perfectly. To eliminate some of the singers, an accompanist might even play just a few high notes to see who can hit them. Singers cannot be shy about warming up by vocalizing in a washroom or the main lobby, if no warmup room is provided. Chances are you will not be the only one walking down the hall singing.

Notices for dancers will state a preference for pointe, jazz, tap, hip-hop, and other forms of dance and movement. Height and age requirements are common. Like singers, dancers are usually expected to bring taped music and to arrive for an audition in time to warm up beforehand. In addition to their prepared routines, they are often expected to learn and execute a new combination taught at the audition.

Hot interpretations of cold readings

Just as dancers may be asked to perform a new combination at an audition, actors, singers, and musicians may be asked to perform a scene or piece they have not practiced. Professionals must do more than just "get through" these cold theatrical readings and musical sight readings, they need to add interpretation. They devote what little preparation time they have to scanning the entire script or piece. Rather than just saying words and hitting notes, they make an effort to perform meaningful phrases.

While it is not possible to practice the actual material used for a cold or sight reading, actors and singers *can* practice the process. Get in the habit of picking up a script or piece of sheet music that you have never seen, scanning, and performing. At the actual audition, lack of soundproofing often gives waiting performers who can overhear what is going on in the audition room a bit more time to think about their own approaches.

Luck can also play a leading role in the cold reading process. I once was handed "sides" from *Gypsy* the day after I saw Bette Midler in the play on television. In his book *Footnotes*, a reference listed in Appendix B, Tony-award-winning dancer and director Tommy Tune tells how he was called back for a singing audition after he passed the dancing audition for a show Jule Styne was producing for the opening of Caesars Palace in Las Vegas. When he finished singing, "You Gotta Have Heart," Styne asked him to do another number. Since Tune only had brought sheet music for the piece he planned to sing, he asked the accompanist if he could play "Time After Time." When the pianist said he could not, Styne volunteered. After all, he had written it.

Make up your own audition, improvise

Actors can expect improvisation to be part of the audition process when they try out for roles that require them to interact with the public. You probably have talked to performers playing parts at theme parks, Renaissance Faires, and historical sites. I used my ad lib skills working as a Phanstormer at Phillies' games and as one of Santa's elves at Macy's. No script tells you how to help a nun celebrate her 49th birthday at the ballpark or how to help a young child wait in line for 45 minutes.

Stripped to its essence, improvisation requires an actor to make up a story based on a given situation. Getting started is the first improv hurdle. After a session, I have had actors ten years my senior thank me for beginning the process. Once begun, the trick is to avoid saying anything negative to stop the action. Watch Robin Williams at work. He has the improv knack of layering one outrageous idea on top of another.

The more you do improv, the more you develop your own technique, whether it is playing the naive maiden, the bully, the snob, or the fool, or acting on the wrong meaning of a word. Just as thin doors give actors, singers, and musicians a chance to overhear cold and sight readings, try to hear what the improv groups called before you are being asked to do. Prior knowledge of a situation gives you more time to develop your original theme.

Turn the callback into the role

One audition may not be enough to land a role. Actors can be called back to read for a part again and again. Additional screen tests may check how you come across on tape or film. I had my first stage kiss playing scenes with different actors to see whose chemistry looked right. Through it all, actors need to rely on the skills they use to sustain fresh theatrical performances night after night in the same play. Keeping the same look—maybe even wearing the same clothes—for every callback is important, too.

Submitting myself over and over again to another's subjective judgment does not top my list of fun things to do, but I remind myself of something Jay Leno said in his book, *Leading with My Chin*, which is included in Appendix B. He figured that without doing a thing, he had moved up the show business ladder every time a guy gave up sitting on the curb waiting all day for his chance to perform at a comedy club. In the same way, those who persevere through a series of callbacks move ahead of those who do not. They also learn their strengths and weaknesses. This is no small benefit. As Brian O'Neil writes in *Acting as a Business*, a book listed in Appendix B, happy, successful actors know themselves. They have a grip on what they do best and where their star shines in the show business galaxy.

When you learn about an audition, often you are alone reading a newspaper or talking to an agent or manager on the telephone. You can visualize yourself giving the role your all. When you go to an audition, you are no longer alone. There might be ten eager candidates in the room. There might be hundreds lined up in the mall or a continuous flow of actors moving past a receptionist into the audition room. When faced with that kind of competition, the challenge is to keep your confidence and composure. I always tell myself: If I fail to land this role, I want everyone to like me and remember me for the next one.

Chapter 8: Live, In Person

Theatre • Theme Parks • One-Man & One-Woman Shows

Chances are we all broke into show business by providing live entertainment. We performed in dance recitals, school plays, holiday pageants, church choirs, and backyard puppet shows. We told knock-knock jokes, tried magic tricks, played our recorders, twirled batons, and demonstrated our gymnastic, karate, and figure skating skills. As time went by, we discovered that we not only liked the spotlight, laughs, and applause, but we also liked rehearsals, painting sets, making costumes, putting on makeup, and wearing wigs. We enjoyed the camaraderie of the players, the pit, and the crew. There was nothing like putting on a show. Each of us began to wonder, "Could I have a stage career?"

Local plays launch professional careers

For most, the chasm between the school stage and Broadway is too wide to leap with a single bound. Theatre lore talks about the small time and the big time. There are an amazing number of small time venues where young actors can gain experience and develop confidence close to home before they begin to audition in major media centers, the big time. As I have discussed, I began my professional training and non-school acting stints in and around my own community.

In particular, I found that summer programs provided both enjoyable vacation activities and a way to work toward my theatrical goal. When I was in elementary school, Mom would call arts centers, theatres, colleges, and summer attractions in early spring to see what summer programs they were planning for young people. Looking through the brochures we received, we could study available activities, dates, and prices. Through the years, I learned juggling, tumbling, and other circus arts; studied dance and band; performed scenes from plays and wrote my own performance material.

The summer after I turned 12, we received a schedule of programs at Longwood Gardens, a public estate west of Philadelphia. According to the flier, the Missoula Children's Theatre (MCT) would be auditioning young people for a production of *Alice in Wonderland* to be performed in the Gardens' open-air theatre. For over 25 years, MCT has been sending teams of two professional actors around the country to stage musical productions, using up to 50 local youngsters at each performance location. Young people, aged five to 18, audition for roles as leads, extras, and dancers in classic stories, such as *Pinocchio, Cinderella, The Pied Piper*, and *Snow White*. Older students, chosen to serve as assistant directors, help with rehearsals, lights, sets, and props.

The Missoula Children's Theatre is an excellent resource available to young actors in small communities and large metropolitan areas. Students from Arizona to Nebraska to Connecticut can be on the lookout for an MCT visit, because the company travels to 40 cities in 20 states each summer and to nearly every state and some Canadian provinces annually. To obtain a travel date schedule and also to learn how to go about sponsoring an MCT stop in your town, contact the troupe's headquarters, listed under Sources in Appendix B.

During my MCT experience, I had a week's run in *Pinocchio* as Catnip Kate the Cat at Longwood Gardens, when I was 13. Going through the auditioning process, a week of rehearsals, and two performances, complete with costumes and makeup, I was totally on my own. Those who knew nothing about my abilities and personality were not going to make allowances for my sensitivities. Constrained by time and budget, everyone associated with the production had a job to do. For me, meeting a new director, actors, musicians, technical people, and wardrobe and makeup assistants was not unlike being the new kid in the four schools I had attended as my mother moved from one college teaching assignment to another. I knew it was up to me to go up to people and say, "Hi, I'm Annie."

One tricky aspect of joining a new cast in teen years and beyond is relationships with actors of the opposite sex. No matter how close a couple becomes during a production, circumstances change as soon as the wrap party ends. By knowing you both will move on to other activities, you can form realistic emotional expectations at the start.

When I was looking for summer acting opportunities two years after my Missoula Children's Theatre experience, I saw an article about the combined auditions I discussed in Chapter Seven. Possibly the most encouraging aspect of attending my first combined audition was the eye-opening realization that a great many theatres, theme parks, outdoor dramas, and other venues hire young people as apprentices, interns, and paid performers. At these auditions, actors, singers, dancers, and crew, even if they have neither an agent nor a union card, can find summer jobs in the theatre.

With luck, a young actor's summer acting experience can lead to other opportunities throughout the year. At one combined audition, I met a recruiter who represented Hedgerow Theatre, which was founded outside Philadelphia by New York actor Jasper Deeter more than 70 years ago. On my resume the recruiter saw that I had taken an acting course at Hedgerow the previous summer. He invited me to try out for the role of Muriel in *Ah, Wilderness!* I had two callbacks but did not land the part. Then, a year and a half later, Hedgerow invited me to audition for a role I did get, in *A Christmas Carol.*

At Hedgerow Theatre, it has become a holiday tradition for some families to place their children in *A Christmas Carol* year after year. Just as annual productions of *The Nutcracker* provide performance opportunities for ballet students, at least half of all LORT theatres (companies in the League of Resident Theatres) offer young actors roles in December productions of *A Christmas Carol,* or some other seasonal classic.

Many of the theatres that participate in combined auditions are listed in the *Regional Theatre Directory,* one of the most reassuring books a young performer can own. This reference book (see Appendix B) lists 450 regional and dinner theatres throughout the United States. Updated annually, the directory gives a brief history of each theatre, summarizes hiring procedures, and lists pay scales and titles of plays produced in the past and planned for the future.

Your first objective should be to get on the mailing lists of nearby regional theatres. That way you will find out, probably in May or over the summer, what plays are planned for next season. When forthcoming plays have roles for young performers, call to see if theatres plan to hold auditions for local actors. Chances are good that they will, because casting nearby youngsters who are under 18 eliminates the need to provide housing for a parent and a tutor.

The *Regional Theatre Directory* tells performers to whose attention their picture/resumes should be addressed at each theatre. If you do not have such names for community and other theatres near you, call and ask for the information. Then, list these names in your files and send headshots and postcard follow-ups.

By developing a relationship with local theatres before your audition, you can improve your chances of being cast in a role. Begin by attending productions at community, regional, summer stock, and dinner theatres. Check programs to find out about future plays and the backgrounds of current performers. Read reviews in local papers. Incorporate relevant information in the cover letters you send with your picture/resumes. Build on these beginning relationships by writing with favorable comments after you see a play and by inviting directors to see your local performances.

Be on the lookout for audition notices in local papers. Thanks to seeing such a notice, I played my first Shakespearean role. To perform in *The Tempest* as a member of the West Chester and Barleysheaf Players, I went through the usual two-minute monologues, cold readings, and callbacks before being cast as Ceres and the understudy for Ariel. Working with this cost-conscious community theatre, I also had opportunities to sew costumes, paint sets, and do my own makeup. Once I had paid dues to join this membership company, I no longer had to keep a keen eye out for its newspaper casting notices. I began receiving newsletters that listed audition dates for future shows.

Some community, regional, and dinner theatres never have to advertise for performers. They cast their shows by using actors already in their files. Taking classes at these theatres, attending combined auditions, and sending mailings to the right people are some of the best ways to get into these files. Also, young actors can begin assembling a valuable network of contacts by keeping in touch with the producers, directors, actors, and others they meet in local theatrical productions. After *The Tempest*, cast members have continued to attend one another's new performances and to share information about auditions for plays and films.

Once you are in a local production, it is time to get some added mileage from your performance. You can package your experience to show that you are the kind of active actor that agents will want to represent. Collect reviews from local papers, playbills, publicity photos, tapes of play snippets shown on local cable stations, and other samples in your portfolio.

Even before you get a chance to show your book to an agent at an interview, send agents publicity photo postcards and quotes from your reviews. Published reviews will give you professional credibility. In particular, send postcards announcing any awards a local theatre gives you and tuck in your portfolio any feature articles written about your prize. If need be, send news releases to generate these stories. Many awards given to actors by various theatre communities around the country are listed in *Back Stage*, where agents read about the winners. Postcards and publicity help bridge the gap between local shows and a wider theatrical audience.

Actors animate theme parks and events

In long-running shows, new actors often replace cast members who go on to other commitments. Theme parks, seasonal productions, annual conventions, the Radio City Rockettes, historical sites, and ice shows are just some of the performance venues that share the characteristics of a long run. They generate a constant demand for new talent. Someone has to suit up as Mickey Mouse at Disneyland, Santa at Macy's, and The Phillie Phanatic mascot at Veterans Stadium. When actors are needed on this kind of continuing basis, a personnel bureaucracy can take hold, because the same hiring procedures are repeated year after year. Actors can expect to submit employment applications along with their picture/resumes.

The *Summer Theatre Directory*, a publication listed in Appendix B, is published annually in December to provide actors with audition dates and other particulars involved in finding employment not just in regular summer stock theatres but also in theme parks, Renaissance Faires, Shakespearean festivals, outdoor dramas, and other summer events. Outdoor amphitheatres in at least 30 states employ actors in all kinds of dramas, from Shakespeare to pageants depicting local history and/or religious events.

Andy Griffith is among the many actors who have performed in *The Lost Colony* by Paul Eliot Green, a musical drama that began running in Manteo, North Carolina, in 1937. College students and generation after generation of local residents take to the stage each summer in religious blockbusters, such as South Dakota's *Black Hills Passion Play* and the *Mormon Miracle Pageant* in Manti, Utah. More than 80 actors bring *TEXAS* to life at the base of a mountain in Canyon, Texas. Young singers thrill a Bardstown, Kentucky, audience with 50 songs from *The Stephen Foster Story.* Actors as well as sword fighters, vocalists, and instrumentalists perform outdoors each summer from Berkeley, California, to Westerly, Rhode Island, in close to 100 Shakespearean festivals.

Recruiting for theme parks, Renaissance faires, and the like often takes place at combined auditions where summer theatres cast their productions. Other auditions are also advertised in theatrical publications like *Back Stage.* One such casting notice for the Radio City Rockettes invites women between 5'5" and 5'9" who are proficient in tap and jazz and are at least 18 years old to audition for the Christmas show. Renaissance faires advertise for a wide variety of talent: actors, singers, dancers, storytellers, magicians, jugglers, strolling musicians, fire eaters, sword swallowers, acrobats, clowns, mimes, animal acts, equestrians, stilt walkers, unicycle riders, and puppeteers.

Each season, Busch Gardens, Opryland, and ice shows send a talent-scouting tour to a dozen or more cities, where audition notices all run in local papers. You can get information about regional, California, and Florida auditions for Disneyland by calling (714) 781-0111 and for Disney World by calling (407) 397-3220. Before I ever saw HERSHEYPARK advertise for performers in a local paper, I simply asked one of the singers at the Park's Minetown Pasta House how she got her job. You can take the same direct approach if you want to become an entertainer at football half-time shows, aquariums, zoos, water shows, mystery dinners, and other live entertainment venues.

Theme park and other vacation, recreation, and holiday audiences are there to have a good time, not a deep theatrical experience. Consequently, your audition appearance and choice of material have to be appropriately upbeat. All monologues, whether contemporary or classical, should be funny and animated. Besides an engaging personality, versatility is prized. Song and dance selections should demonstrate an ability to handle different styles—perhaps 16 bars of an up-tempo song and ballad and a dance combination that includes tap and jazz. Stamina is also important. No old injuries should kick up when you need to put on a production number five days a week, sometimes several times a day.

In contrast to the upbeat performance expected at entertainment venues, teaching hospitals and law schools hire actors to play sobering roles. Once performers are briefed on the facts of a case and information about their character, they help law schools and law firms teach young attorneys how to take complaints from potential legal clients and how to handle witnesses at a trial. In medical schools actors perform as "standardized patients." While a videotape rolls, student and foreign doctors try to pass clinical tests by questioning actors who have mastered scripts covering their characters' medical symptoms and family histories.

Pay may be by the week, day, or hour. In the late 1990's, for example, theme parks paid anywhere from $250 to $1,000 for a 5-day, 35- to 50-hour week. Most performers made about $350 a week, and contracts could run from six months to a year. By the day, the pay range was $80 to $120. I made $40 a game at the ballpark. Hourly wages were in the $7 to $12 range. Transportation, housing expenses, and costumes may or may not be covered. Depending on the venue, possible perks are: medical, dental, and vision benefits; paid holidays; complimentary tickets; tuition reimbursement;

free acting, voice, and dance classes; merchandise discounts; a chance to audition for television shows and films shot in the area; and a profit-sharing plan.

One man or woman alone in the spotlight

In almost direct contrast to large productions in theme parks, outdoor dramas, and musical revues that interchangeably plug many different performers into the same show year after year, the entertainment field includes stand-up comedians, cabaret singers, and other solo performers who develop and book their own acts.

I grew up watching such a performer begin by practicing on his unicycle. By the time he was in high school, he had created his own summer job. Adding jokes, juggling, magic, and balloon animals to his unicycle tricks, he played neighborhood birthday parties, retirement homes, fairs, festivals, and day-care centers. Although he continues to perform occasionally, after graduating from college his skill booking his own act led him into a career as a business manager for several musical groups.

Live entertainers who write, perform, and book their own acts expand their show business opportunities. Writing can propel a career into many directions. A member of Britain's Monty Python comedy group, Eric Idle, is now the author of the book for the Dr. Seuss musical, *The Seussical.*

Television provides many examples of the solo-performer route to success, especially by comedians. Former stand-up stars host late-night talk shows and create characters and sketches for *Saturday Night Live.* I still remember seeing a hilarious, one-woman "Valley Girl" routine by Whoopi Goldberg. Producers prowl comedy clubs hoping to find more sitcom characters like Tim Allen, Roseanne, Cosby, or Seinfeld. HBO is famous for featuring one-person comedy specials by the likes of Chris Rock and Tracey Ullman.

Carmine DeSena's book *The Comedy Market* provides invaluable guidance for young actors thinking about rooting their entertainment careers in an ability to be funny. As the title of his book implies, DeSena does not tell how to develop characters or write jokes, sketches, or sitcoms, but he does offer practical suggestions for selling comedy creations. Over and over again, he stresses the importance of observation and information.

If local comedy clubs and colleges have open mikes, stop in and get to know the audience and who books acts. Giving your own performances at school or church talent shows, senior centers, and hospitals will be good practice and reveal ways to improve. Just as friends and family help individual athletes perfect their skills by videotaping performances on the field, friends and relatives can tape a young comedian's act in various venues. Much can be learned by watching a routine and listening to an audience's reaction.

Once you begin to look for solo performers, you will see numerous examples. Shari Lewis and her puppets won 12 Emmy Awards. Coming from very different directions, Richard Simmons, Martha Stewart, and Arnold Schwarzenegger turned doing their own things into entertainment successes. You may hear a storyteller at a school assembly or see a performer dress and talk like George Washington the way Hal Holbrook used to dress and talk like Mark Twain. Then, there are those Elvis impersonators! I once read about Ruth Draper, a solo performer who spent her career creating characters on stage; she died after a performance at age 72. By refining their own originality, it seems actors can create their own lifetime warranties.

I have heard it said that live entertainment is an actor's art, while television and film are a director's. The actor has nothing to do with how a scene is shot, cut, or assembled. Once a TV series or movie is finished, it is static, ready to view over and over again, unchanged. Appearing live, actors never know what will happen in a play, theme park show, or comedy club gig. There is always the chance to be great.

Chapter 9: Small Screen and Big

Commercials • Television Shows • Films

Remember Mikey! Not only did he like Life cereal, but he also made bowls full of money. Agents and managers love to book young actors in commercials, television shows, and films. When a client is cast as a principal, as opposed to an extra in background shots, an agent earns a commission on the *residuals*—payment an actor receives every time a commercial airs. Actors who are regulars on soap operas may work for years. Cast members in a popular television series and in films reap the benefits from worldwide distribution, reruns, and home video sales. Young actors have a major advantage if they live near New York City or Los Angeles, where advertising agencies, television and film studios, and production companies are concentrated.

Get real about commercials

Students who begin their show business careers with a role in their school musicals may need a course in on-camera techniques before they audition for their first television commercial. I found such a class at a modeling agency, but local casting directors, acting schools, and colleges also offer these courses. The first time I tried to sell a product on camera, my teacher asked, "Have you done a lot of theatre?" When on camera, I learned, you do not have to project to the back row of the balcony. Words need to flow naturally and not be enunciated one by one. Grand stage reactions detract from the product and the sale. Camera closeups reveal nuances as well as unwanted eye blinking, head bobbing, swaying, and lip biting or licking.

Besides toning down voices and performances, commercial acting classes also help students get used to seeing themselves on television. The first time I could watch myself on a monitor as I was being taped at an audition, all I kept thinking was, "My head is enormous!" Commercials strive for reality and credibility, qualities that relaxed actors project when they are comfortable in front of a camera, speaking directly to their new best friends out there in television land.

Much has been written about the kind of television performers and performances people want to see on shows and commercials viewed in their homes. Leo Burnett in Chicago is one of the biggest ad agencies searching for actors with an acceptable, clean-cut, all-American look. Along with blue-eyed blonds with clear skin and engaging smiles, the public also wants to see freckle-faced redheads, African-Americans, Asians, Hispanics, and other ethnic actors who reflect the diversity of the population and the sponsor's consumers.

Simply by watching television commercials you can get a good feel for the nerds, popular girls, mousy friends, jocks, women's libbers, bad boys, ladies' men, and chubby types of young actors in demand. You also will see skateboarding, rollerblading, basketball, swimming, horseback riding, and other sports used in commercials. If these passions are yours, make sure you include them in the Special Skills section of your resume. They may be the reason an agent recommends you for an audition.

No matter how perfect your look and talents are for a commercial, at an audition you have to be professional to land the part. That means never being late, always bringing picture/resumes, taking direction pleasantly, not chewing gum, and being cooperative, flexible, friendly, polite, and clean. Pay attention to the names of the people holding the audition, from the receptionist to the person behind the camera to the director. Ask a question or two about the product, situation, or your character. Listen to the answers and use the information in your performance.

Since having the right look is the difference between landing and not landing a commercial, actors have to go to an audition with a bag full of quick change magic. By arriving early enough to see the script and the other actors in the waiting room, you can judge what type of character is needed. Along with the makeup, extra pairs of socks, bottles of water, and nutrition bars in your bag, you might carry barrettes, eyeglass frames, a temporary tattoo, a vest, tie, bandana, hat, flower, bobby pins, hair spray, stethoscope, stuffed animal, clipboard, and any other item you have practiced using to change your look.

During one on-camera practice class, all seven of us were asked to demonstrate unmanageable hair for a conditioner commercial. Gamely, we pretended to comb the tangles out of our hair. Surveying the scene, our teacher asked, "Don't any of you have a comb? This isn't a mime class," he stated. I learned my lesson. Commercials aim for reality, and that includes *real* props.

When making a commercial, young actors should strive to be principals who are clearly seen and/or heard. Principals are the actors who receive residual payments when a commercial is reused.

Defined in a number of ways, principals can be "foreground identifiable" in a closeup or when they deliver lines, show a product, react to what someone says off-camera, or perform a stunt. The back of a head does not count. Actors who are not seen can be considered principals only when they are heard delivering dialogue in voice-overs.

My one and only performance in a television commercial did not qualify me for residuals. As a "Phanstormer" at Philadelphia Phillies baseball games, my job included giving away prizes and squirting fans with a Super Soaker at "Bleacher Beach." When the Phillies made a commercial featuring this new promotional playground, the cameraman asked me to shoot some water at him. Too bad I did not take off my sunglasses! I could tell everyone to watch for me in the next Phillies' commercial, but I was far from "foreground identifiable."

Anywhere there is an advertising agency, there is an opportunity to be cast in a television commercial. Someone is making those television ads for local car dealers, banks, appliance and furniture stores, hospitals, and Realtors. By calling an agency and saying you are a local actor, you can find out how to submit your picture/resume for casting consideration. Outside New York, Los Angeles and Chicago, payments to actors in commercials are determined by population and the number of uses. Rates drop like a stone in smaller markets compared to payments for commercials shown in the three major markets and on every network-affiliated station throughout the country.

TV show guidance

One of my favorite diversions is watching celebrities on talk shows. I like hearing what they did before they became famous. Harrison Ford took out library books to teach himself carpentry. Danny DeVito was a hairdresser. Most of all, I like observing what makes guests interesting. They have stories to tell and they know how to tell them. They choose attention-getting outfits, adjust their ties and cuff links, lean on a hand, rub an arm, smooth and toss their hair, wink, look amazed, and smile. Television producers and directors are looking for people like this who know how to command attention.

The outgoing, spontaneous personality of Kirstie Alley, the unique look and voice of Jaleel White's Steve Urkel, and the creative, funny improv turns of Michael Richards all help make television shows, as well as television commercials, memorable. Agents and managers who represent actors with that little something extra send their clients to L.A. every year for "pilot season," the mid-January to June ritual when sample television shows are cast and produced for the fall.

Before you go West to audition, you can sample the TV show environment by being part of a live talk, game, sitcom, or late-night show audience. Network addresses you can use to request television show tickets are in Appendix B. Far more important than the unlikely possibility that you will be seen on television at one of these broadcasts is the opportunity for you to see a TV studio at work. Lights, cameras, cue cards, applause signs, stage manager, makeup artists, and the preshow warmup will become part of your mind's database. You never know when being able to make an intelligent comment, based on your television audience experience, will give you a professional edge.

On *The Tonight Show with Jay Leno*, I remember hearing Billy Crystal tell how he used to come to Manhattan to be in television audiences for the sole purpose of coughing right before the show went to a commercial. "That's me," he could tell his friends when they heard his last-minute hacking.

I myself had an interesting experience at *Late Night with Conan O'Brien*. Mom and I went to his show the first time when I was 16, the minimum age for audience members. We saw people lining up a couple of hours ahead of the 4:30 p.m. taping and joined the queue. Shortly after we were seated in the studio, O'-Brien came out, ran up the stairs into the audience, and began dancing with a woman seated on the aisle.

When we went back to *Late Night with Conan O'Brien* the next year, I aimed for one of the aisle seats where O'Brien was most likely to look for a guest willing to participate in the preshow warmup. Things did not go exactly as planned. When one student in the audience said that he was a chemistry major, the announcer asked other students to call out their majors. Obviously, I shouted, "Theatre!" Somehow things got out of hand. Asked what college I attended, I said that I was still in high school in Pennsylvania. Suddenly I was labeled a runaway just in from the bus terminal. At least I had a brief moment in the television studio spotlight.

Luck was responsible for my first real television show appearance. While I was working as an elf in Macyland during the holiday season, *Access Hollywood* decided to do a segment showing soap opera dads celebrating Christmas with their children. When Frank Dicopoulos from *Guiding Light* brought his family to Macyland, I was the on-camera elf who said, "Welcome to Santa's Village, right this way." In truth, this was not my first TV appearance. I had been on a number of *Wayne's World*-type public access programs that my high school beamed into the community. During band concert broadcasts, I was seen playing clarinet solos.

Young actors might well explore the possibility of developing their own material, writing a proposal, and pitching their ideas for a program, interview, or segment to a local cable company. My mother is a member of an organization that got a weekly program using that approach. Call the station manager's secretary to find out if the cable company has any submission guidelines and to ask whom you should talk to about your suggestions. If the station is interested in your proposal, suddenly you will have a producer, technical studio support, and material to make one terrific demo tape. If you decide that your future lies in packaging your own material, the process for approaching a network or production company is much the same as what you will have done to launch your career on public access television.

Industrial films educate and entertain

As foreign-language students, we have seen films and tapes that introduced us to other cultures. At work, our parents see training films and tapes that inform them about their health benefits. On airplanes, we all have seen videos showing how a carry-on bag must fit under the seat. These are all examples of industrial films.

If there are a number of government agencies, major corporations, or trade associations in your area, they could be using nearby locations for sales, training, product demonstration, and benefit presentation films. You may find that a local independent casting director is handling auditions for the production companies making these industrial films, or you may have to call the government offices, companies, and associations directly. Ask if any films are planned and who is responsible for supervising their production.

Appearing in industrial films provides useful training for young actors. One day on location certainly offers a good introduction to everything involved in the movie-making art. When I was eight, I had my first film experience in an industrial film made for the Pennsylvania Teachers' Retirement Fund. Mom had seen a notice for extras posted on the bulletin board at a college where she was teaching. A California production company was using the arboretum next to the college as the setting for the retirement fund film.

When Mom and I arrived at the arboretum at 8:00 a.m., we drove around and around until we found one car parked near a meadow. It belonged to another extra. Cars and trucks continued to arrive during the next two hours. The cameraman sticks out in my memory, because he wore a stereotypical movie mogul's black beret. Adult actors went through a dry rehearsal before the cameras started to roll. I needed no rehearsal. There was nothing complicated about my character's motivation. I was a carefree eight-year-old kid playing a carefree eight-year-old kid playing with a ball. Cameras were positioned. Sound levels were check-ed. Once, I was hit in the nose with the ball. The day was cold and getting colder. I often went back to the car to get warm. Sandwiches were ordered for lunch. By 3:30 p.m. we were finished and everyone packed up to leave.

Ups and downs of student films

By the time I had reached high school, we had begun subscribing to *Back Stage*. Student filmmakers often use this publication to advertise for ac-tors. In response to such an ad, I sent a letter and pic-ture/resume to a student making a senior thesis film at New York University. She invited me to audition. For-tunately, Amtrak was running a special 2-tickets-for-1 promotion. Mom and I were grateful for the savings, be-cause we would make four trips to New York in the next month.

My audition was a success. I had some-thing in common with the producer, who also had at-tended Philadelphia's High School for the Creative and Performing Arts, and I impressed the filmmaker with an improvisation. As Mary, the lead, I would be an innocent Catholic girl who spent the entire movie frantically hiding in everyone else's shadow until I shot and killed another girl at the end. In the improv, I was asked to pretend that I just hit a squirrel with my car.

I began by singing "Amazing Grace" as I mimed steering the car and ended in tears saying the Lord's Prayer over the invisible roadkill. My improv was such a hit that I eventually sang a Calypso version of "Amazing Grace" over the film's opening credits. The movie itself, titled *The Shack*, was supposed to capture the gory ruin that passes for friendship among adoles-cent girls. A camping trip brought together the tomboy, the sex kitten, the chubby, and me, the born-again Christian. The macabre film dripped with fake blood and oozing red nail polish, and featured a skull, an axe mur-der, a beheading, and a spirited Ouija board. There was still time to find out who got her period first and last and who stole whose boyfriend.

Filming was scheduled for ten days in October on location in Connecticut. At the producer's expense, we took up residence in a motel. Rain ruined the schedule for outdoor shots, and one day rain dripped through a hole in the shack's roof and into a light setting off sparks. We were sure we were all about to be electrocuted.

Thankfully, we survived, and in January we went to New York University to see raw footage of *The Shack*. All five takes of one scene were out of focus and completely worthless. Another scene was too dark to identify the actors by anything other than their voices. A professor said the out-of-focus scene could be reshot on a campus sound stage and the dark camping scene could be filmed in Central Park. A student told me I was a good actress. Based on this film, no one else will ever know. Both *The Shack* and its disillusioned filmmaker disappeared from New York University.

By the time I made my next NYU student film I was living in New York. Transportation involved only a subway ride to a prep school location on the Upper East Side. One of the best things about student films is the fact that they nearly always have roles appropriate for young actors. College screenwriters work with subjects they know.

Another fringe benefit of performing in student films is the good habits you develop for future projects. You get to know the crew by name and learn to respect the importance of lighting, camerawork, sound, and the other technical crafts involved. While rolling with the punches of filming scenes out of sequence, you become attentive to the need to maintain costume, prop, and other logical aspects of continuity. When you are hired for a feature film, your student film experience will have prepared you to arrive with the instincts of a professional.

Breaking into feature film

The summer after I turned 16, a *Back Stage* casting notice for *Sleepers* caught my attention. I had just finished reading the book, and here was an item saying Robert De Niro and Brad Pitt were scheduled to star in the film. A casting director was looking for teenage extras to be in a twist contest scene as well as for cars from the 1970s to provide authenticity in outdoor shots. I knew how to do the twist, and I had just passed my driver's test and inherited my cousin's 1979 Toyota. I went to New York with enthusiasm. My confidence flagged a bit when I saw blocks and blocks of potential extras waiting to turn in their headshots. Room after room of candidates filled and emptied as staff passed out and collected questionnaires. Although I mentioned the twist and the Toyota, I was never called for the film.

Yes, I was disappointed, but I realized that the long lines and low probability of landing a role at an open call were not unusual. What good would it do to resent everyone who failed to see how right I was for the role? It seemed to me that actors who lived in New York could attend open calls or not depending on what other prospects and obligations they had for the day. If they landed a part, fine; if not, they incurred no major commitment of time or extra transportation costs. Here was another reason to move to New York. After I did move, I finally was an extra, in James Gardiner's independent film, *A Pleasant Shade of Gray*. One weekend, I had to be on the set at 4:30 a.m. on Saturday and at 5:30 a.m. on Sunday. That is not the kind of schedule you can handle if you are traveling into the city from another state.

Outside New York and Hollywood, some cities and states have established government offices designed to attract movie companies. *Up Close and Personal, Beloved, 12 Monkeys,* and *Snake Eyes* are just a few of the films that were shot in the Philadelphia area while I lived there. Philadelphia's film office has a hotline that provides weekly updates listing casting directors and production companies looking for area acting, technical, and administrative personnel.

To see if any films are scheduled to be shot in your area, check the monthly listing in *Ross Reports Television & Film.* Besides New York and California, you will see casting opportunities in Arizona, Atlanta, Florida, North Carolina, Washington, D.C., Iowa, Texas, and many other locations. If you live nearby, call the production company listed and ask who will handle local casting.

In the cover letter you send with your picture/resume, say that you live in the area. You will not be the only resident eager to appear in a feature film, however, and the producer may advertise for extras in local papers. In Twin Falls, Idaho, over 2,700 people had to be screened in 1998 for 700 extra parts in *Breakfast of Champions* with Bruce Willis. As often happens, some successful extras did have their parts upgraded to speaking roles and more screen time.

Whatever film work you can find, all of it—in commercials, television, and film—is raw material for a well-edited demo tape that will convince agents, managers, casting directors, and producers that you have the perfect look and experience to book future projects.

Chapter 10: Where Do I Go to School?

B.A. • B.F.A. • Conservatory • Coach

From preschool to high school, annual musicals showcase budding actors and dancers. Drama teachers often enter their students in one-act play contests and distribute applications for summer honors programs. Magnet high schools in New York, Washington, Philadelphia, and other cities nurture the talents of students in the creative and performing arts. Young actors experience no shortage of material or motivation for the personal essays college applications require. What we want to do in the future is clear. We can explain why getting a laugh is our greatest accomplishment and outline the steps we took to overcome a weakness like stage fright.

Unfortunately, high school guidance offices offer little help to seniors who wish to continue their dramatic training. I am not sure my counselor ever believed The Juilliard School does not require SAT scores. Since advisers *do* see the Arts Recognition and Talent Search (ARTS) awards mentioned in the computerized lists of scholarships that they receive, guidance counselors often do urge young actors to apply for these prizes.

In addition to the opportunity to win financial aid for college, there are many reasons to request an ARTS application from the National Foundation for Advancement in the Arts, an organization listed under Sources in Appendix B. The ARTS competition is judged by directors and other theatre people in a position to help a young actor's career. Also, students are asked to submit a videotaped audition. If you do not have a demo tape, here is your motivation and opportunity to find age-appropriate, contrasting monologues and someone to record your performance. You end up with two audition pieces and a way to study how to perfect them, not only for college applications but also for professional auditions. Finally, at your request, the National Foundation for Advancement in the Arts will send your name, as an ARTS contest entrant, to colleges, universities, and conservatories that admit and offer financial aid to young performers.

Money and training will be issues for performers throughout their careers. After high school, one of an actor's main concerns is the need to accumulate professional credits that will impress an agent. This objective suggests the need to look at the real life experience schools provide. Do they place interns in local television studios and film production companies; do they prepare students for combined auditions and/or run their own professional summer stock theatres?

A school's promotional materials often list well-known alumni. What these materials do not say is how much the schools contributed to the success of these actors and how much these actors did on their own. Young performers who have appeared in TV commercials, feature films, and Broadway productions enter college with an agent and professional credits. They can afford to attend Yale or Stanford without amassing an overwhelming student loan burden. In other words, Kellie Martin, Claire Danes and Fred Savage are not role models to be imitated blindly by students who graduate from high school with no such professional experience or nest egg. My objective in this chapter is to help you think about your post-high school options and to help you make choices that are right for you.

Deciding among B.A., B.F.A., or Conservatory Programs

According to the *Directory of Theatre Training Programs*, listed in Appendix B, more than 400 colleges, universities, and conservatories offer courses to prepare professional actors.

Liberal arts colleges granting Bachelor of Arts (B.A.) degrees require students to complete an academic core curriculum, no matter what their major. SAT scores, not auditions, are among the factors considered for admission. Theatre majors in a B.A. program probably will not have any internship requirements for graduation, and they may have an opportunity to perform only in extracurricular productions.

With less competition from serious acting students, it may be easier to land the lead in a play or musical at a liberal arts college than at a conservatory, for example. Yet, student actors should not expect their liberal arts schools to invite agents to these productions. Independently, drama students can use a directory, such as the *Summer Theatre Directory* (listed in Appendix B), to find summer theatre or training programs to augment their professional preparation. Another consideration: students who choose to work toward a B.A. often want a fallback career option—in education or computer science, for example.

Students pursuing Bachelor of Fine Arts (B.F.A.) degrees expect to receive intense theatrical training and career support from their schools. Compared to that of B.A. programs, the required core academic curriculum is much smaller. Most time is spent studying various aspects of acting and working on student productions. Auditions usually are required for admission and periodic faculty reviews determine who continues in the program. (Bear in mind that these evaluations can be as subjective as those of a figure-skating judge. A school may decide, for example, that it has too many leading men or not enough minority students.)

Since faculty members in a B.F.A. program often are chosen for their professional credentials, they tend to have personal relationships with working agents, directors, and producers whom they bring in as guest speakers and invite to showcases designed to launch graduating seniors. It is not unusual for students to sign with agents who have seen them at these performances.

Acting conservatories have much in common with B.F.A. programs. Admission is by audition, and faculty reviews determine who stays in the school. Students do not receive a degree, however, because there is little or no academic component in the curriculum. The sole focus is on professional training and employment, normally within a period of two or three years. Spending the day with students and faculty who are focused, almost exclusively, on acting-related classes and the next audition may be too stifling for those who also have other interests, for example, in languages, science, and sports.

The *Directory of Theatre Training Programs* identifies the various degrees offered by hundreds of schools. It also provides basic facts about admission procedures, tuition, and financial aid. By using the directory and catalogues requested from schools that interest you, you can gain eye-opening information about faculty, theatrical productions, and curriculum.

When a B.A. program has only one faculty member in theatre, for example, exposure to acting techniques is going to be limited. Schools that list "Staff" as the professor for undergraduate courses probably put students in the hands of overworked teaching assistants who are graduate students trying to complete their own programs. By looking at a list of recent productions, a potential student can judge if the drama department concentrates on one genre or exposes actors to a full range of classical to contemporary plays.

All actors should see if a school's curriculum offers training in voice and movement along with introductions to theatre, acting, and design. Students who wish to pursue careers in television and film need to investigate a school's record for placing interns in those fields and its policy toward assigning mentors and giving credit for independent study at local studios. Ultimately, a campus visit and talks with faculty, current students, and recent graduates all help develop an overall picture of the subjective experience a beginning actor could expect to have at a school.

Young actors should aspire to experiences similar to the ones Barry Levinson, the director of Oscar-Winning *Rain Man* and Emmy-winning *Homicide: Life on the Street*, had as a student at The American University in Washington, D.C. Thanks to a professor who doubled as a program director at a local television station, Levinson gained practical studio experience at the station. As an apprentice, he watched and studied as many as ten films a week when he was responsible for programming commercial breaks during late-night movies. While he was viewing *Citizen Kane* and *Casablanca* at the station, on campus he was learning to write for an audience. Knowing his creative writing professor would read aloud and classmates would comment on everything he wrote helped Levinson develop skills that later won two comedy writing Emmys for his work on *The Carol Burnett Show*.

Does location count?

A school's faculty can be expected to have most of its contacts in the local market. Through their teachers, acting students in school in New York City, Los

Angeles, Chicago, and London begin to make contacts in the places where theatre, television, and film jobs are concentrated. Cities that house branch offices of entertainment unions (see SAG listing in Apprentix B) are additional centers where actors can carve out a living in commercials, theatre, industrials, voice-overs, comedy clubs, and an occasional film. In entertainment hubs, local agents can come to college productions, student directors from schools in the area are always looking for casts, and local papers are filled with opportunities. Being a student in a major metropolitan area also enables a young actor to ease into the experience of coping with expenses, distractions, intense professional competition, facelessness, and urban dangers.

I have heard about actors trained in wonderful college drama programs far from urban areas that are the centers of arts activities who have gone on to have stellar careers. In my mind, they are the exceptions. If you go through high school and four years of college and no one has seen your work except teachers, friends, and relatives, you are at a disadvantage compared with actors who have trained and learned to audition where most of the jobs are. At schools far from advertising and show business centers, a student must either try to gain experience as an intern in local television or a resident theatre company before attempting to break into the big time, or, like my half brother who is on television in Montana, be willing to build a happy life in a smaller community.

I only requested catalogues from schools in New York City and London. Along with colleges offering B.A. and B.F.A. degrees, I found a number of Manhattan conservatories that were accredited by the National Association of Schools of Theatre (NAST) to receive federal grants and loans.

My list of New York conservatories included:

- The American Academy of Dramatic Arts
- The American Musical & Dramatic Academy
- Circle In The Square Theatre School
- National Shakespeare Conservatory
- Neighborhood Playhouse School of Theatre

- School for Film and Television
- The Stella Adler Conservatory of Acting.

In addition to schools, I also complied a list, which is reprinted in Appendix B, of New York housing options for student actors.

Two free guides helped me explore schools in the country of the bard, as well as of John Gielgud, Anthony Hopkins, and Jonathan Pryce. The Conference of Drama Schools publishes *The Official U.K. Guide to Drama Training*, and British Information Services in New York distributes *Study in Britain*. Both publications, which are listed in Appendix B, provide addresses for drama and film schools. The *U.K. Guide* also itemizes the entry requirements, housing, degrees, and theatre courses at 19 drama schools. (Students who want to sample what the U.K. has to offer might look into the summer programs offered at the schools listed in these same publications.)

I found that some UK schools hold auditions in the U.S., while others require you to go to them. Also, and especially important, of the more than 100 Americans who annually audition for the Royal Academy of Dramatic Art, few receive callbacks. Some years, no U.S. citizens make the final cut. At the London Academy of Performing Arts, however, one-fifth of the enrollment might be from the United States.

Even more than my concern about chances of being admitted to a British school, I had to face the reality of cost and foreign-exchange considerations about the strength of the dollar. U.S. government loans are not readily available for students attending colleges overseas, and permits to work your way through British schools are restricted. Plus, how often would I want to come home? Such trips would add the expense of flying back and forth between the U.S. and Europe.

After checking London off my list, I also eliminated schools that confer B.A. degrees. I knew that I was not interested in a program that required me to take math and science courses unrelated to my career plans. When I sent for my first college catalogues the summer after my freshman year in high school, the only one that said anything about the percentage of its graduates who actually found work in some area of the theatre, television, or the film industry was the catalogue from The Juilliard School.

Early in my senior year of high school, I filled out an application for Juilliard's B.F.A. program and sent in a sizeable fee ($85 at the time). Along with thousands of hopefuls, half in high school and the rest older, who attend Juilliard's annual January and February auditions, I competed for as few as 20 places in the freshman class. I was not chosen to be in "Group XXX," as Juilliard called the class of 2001. Next, I went on to an audition at a New York conservatory, where I had also applied for admission. There, my audition was a success and the school offered a generous financial aid package that would help cover expenses. To fully handle New York's high cost of living, however, I figured I also needed a job.

The prospect of trying to repay college loans with an actor's insecure earnings was never very attractive. I expected costs for tuition, room and board, books and supplies, spring-break vacations, and other college expenses to far outstrip income available from scholarships, parents, and summer and after-school jobs. In fact, I probably would have to work as an *unpaid* intern to accumulate professional experience. Loans that would come due after graduation would limit my options as they had for some of my friends who majored in drama in college. Instead of pursuing an acting career, they have taken jobs as a high-school English teacher, a fund raiser in a theatre's development office, youth minister, community theatre director, and corporate public relations assistant.

As soon as I moved to Manhattan, I began looking for employment. Suddenly, I had auditions to be an elf at Macy's, an extra in an independent film, an actor with lines in a student film, an ingenue in a touring company, and a spokesperson for a manufacturer at a toy fair. I also registered with a temp service that staffs conventions and another that sent me to receptionist positions on Wall Street. I began asking myself a few questions. Was it my location outside Philadelphia that had hampered my career? Instead of entering a school's structured program, could I get a similar amount of experience and training on my own?

Actors learn their craft at colleges and conservatories, but they also study on their own with private coaches. Not to be ignored as well is how much actors learn on the job, working in all aspects of the entertainment business. We are, after all, in a field where coaches and directors coax children into performances that win Oscars, Emmys and Tonys.

Young actors who have confidence to audition and maturity to recognize the areas they need to improve can fashion their own curriculum. Training in a wide variety of entertainment and advertising commercial specialties is available in New York City, Los Angeles, and elsewhere. Local papers often run special fall and summer sections featuring theatre workshops and classes in voice, dance, piano and other instruments. Each week *Back Stage* devotes its last pages to ads for voice, diction, and dialect coaches and for classes in on-camera work, stage combat, scene study, improv, movement, and stand-up comedy. You can attend conferences and summer camps for an introduction to writing and directing plays, films and television shows.

Not every coach or class is right for every actor. Faced with numerous training options, students should expect to devote time and effort to the task of visiting classes and seeking recommendations from other actors and professionals. I was lucky to find my first New York clarinet teacher by speaking to a young woman who was carrying a clarinet case on the bus, and asking her where she took lessons.

Individually tailored training programs, unlike scheduled college and conservatory classes, have the advantage of giving more experienced actors, especially those represented by agents, greater flexibility to attend auditions. Private coaches usually understand that a callback takes priority over a class. They are willing to accommodate an actor's need to reschedule missed sessions, something professors cannot do because they have too many other students to consider.

In New York I also allowed myself to wonder if men and women should think about college differently. As long as the entertainment field sees 30-plus females as "over-the-hill," women have to question the wisdom of spending four of their under-30 years in college. The nature of the industry suggests male actors need not share this view. First of all, in my experience, more women want to be actors than men. Secondly, while only young women are in demand as leading ladies, men from the initially smaller male casting pool seem to enjoy a much longer run. Lost hair and wrinkles have done little to diminish the box-office appeal of Clint Eastwood, Harrison Ford, Robert Redford, Sean Connery, Paul Newman, and Jack Nicholson.

The conclusion may be: male actors can graduate from college and pursue life-long careers. Unless they tend more toward becoming character actresses like *Friends* and film star Lisa Kudrow, female actors may be better advised to attend college and incur heavy-duty, student-loan debt *after* age reduces the number of roles open to them. I decided to drop out of the conservatory before I began. Along with income from my new acting jobs and temp assignments, freed-up tuition money enabled me to cover living expenses and private lessons. Fortunately, my SAT scores and National Honor Society high school record give me the option of attending college, if not next year, then at some point in the future.

Certainly I am not delighted about the stigma attached to being a college dropout. To some people, my failure to register for classes confirmed what they believed about actors in general: they are not too bright. When I told a former boyfriend that I no longer planned to attend college, he actually said, "I do not want people thinking my wife is stupid." Another actor who is himself a college dropout once lectured me on having no focus in my life. I also know to brace myself for lectures from parents of college-educated actors determined to defend the get-that-piece-of-paper advice that they gave their own sons and daughters. Some of my own relatives oppose my decision, and even those who seem to accept it periodically reopen a discussion about my college plans.

Aside from dealing with the perceptions of others, I find that young actors who are not students have other practical concerns. Not only are they ineligible for college health insurance plans, but their parents' health plans may no longer cover them either. Obviously, without a college I.D., young actors cannot take advantage of merchant, transportation, and other student discounts.

In the end, each individual must find his or her own path—and even then, few decisions actors make are final. New factors and opportunities can suggest a different path or challenge a choice of college, conservatory or coach. I have a friend who went through the trouble of attending a university's summer program to make sure that she would like a school's location and what it offered. In her first semester as a freshman, she became disillusioned. Not only was she not permitted to audition for any roles in the university's productions, she learned that freshmen could not even serve as crew members. Another problem that can affect a college experience is faculty turnover. What good is talking to recent graduates and visiting a school, when the entire quality and direction of a department can change, if one professor leaves or a new chair arrives?

Of course, you may not get into the school of your choice, or you may be cut because of poor faculty evaluations after you are admitted. You yourself may decide to leave because you land a role in a television pilot. Robin Williams and Helen Hunt did not hesitate to leave college as soon as they had professional acting options. Later in life, you may decide to throw over your acting career to study law, just as an attorney may decide he really is an actor or politician. As long as students intend to be actors, the best way they can evaluate and re-evaluate their college and conservatory experiences is not in terms of classes taken but in progress toward their professional careers.

Chapter 11: The Care and Feeding of Actors

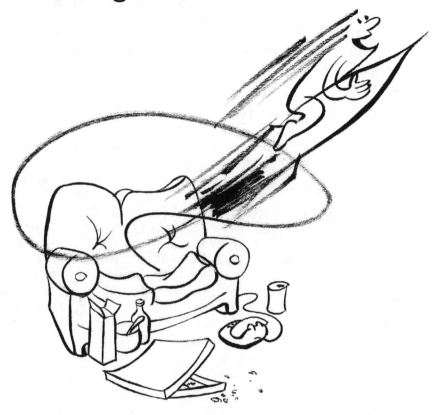

Rejection • Talent Diversification
Sacrifices • Coping Tactics

At an awards dinner, I once ran into a former actor who told me that she had abandoned her theatrical career because she failed to land two parts—the first two parts she ever lost. I, who had been her understudy, cannot begin to count the number of times I have been rejected for a role. Losing a part is painful, whether it is the first time or the hundredth. Being judged from a piece of paper mailed to an agent or as a face, body, or type at an audition takes a toll on the psyche. Sometimes I want to yell, "I'm a complete person!" For me, being a professional means controlling these urges and trying again. My determination may change in time, but quitting show business in my teens would be even more painful than my next rejection. Drawing on the ups and downs I have experienced, I want to share a few useful principles that have kept me going when times were rough.

Look beyond rejection

In my first middle-school performance, I beat out eighth-graders to play the juicy role of The Artful Dodger in *Oliver!* A year later, I ran out of school crying when I saw the cast list for *Bye Bye Birdie*. I was Ursula, a role with exactly two minutes of dialogue. Yes, I actually timed it. To make matters worse, I was double-cast and performed only two nights during the musical's four-night run. Repeating to myself over and over, "There are no small parts," I was determined to recover from the shock. I crafted my scattered seconds on stage into a character that people still mention to me. On closing night, applause for my featured performance toward the end of Act One delayed the next song.

In my first high school play, I had to deal with a slight even worse that being double-cast in a minor role. As an extra, I had *no* lines. By mid-year, however, I auditioned successfully for the High School for the Creative and Performing Arts in Philadelphia.

I began to realize that good things can follow bad just as surely as bad can follow good. To illustrate further, the day after I saw my name was not on a cast list in sophomore year, I received a telephone call inviting me to audition for a student film at New York University. I landed the part. After another failed high school audition, a community theatre gave me my first Shakespearean role. Unsuccessful at my attempt to enter Juilliard, I was accepted by another conservatory. Following a combined audition where no theatre asked for my services, a recruiter from the Philadelphia Phillies invited me to spend my summer at the ballpark as a

Phanstormer. Unable to land a part-time salesclerk position at any of three New York specialty stores, I was hired as a Macy's elf and an extra in an independent film.

Diversify your talents

Looking at someone like Paul Reiser, a stand-up comedian, author, and songwriter who has done films, TV sitcoms, and commercials, you begin to suspect that the more you diversify, the more show business opportunities you can make for yourself. What did Matt Damon and Ben Affleck do when they could not find acting jobs? They wrote parts for themselves in *Good Will Hunting*. Miramax bought their script complete with the condition that Matt and Ben would play the roles they created.

I find ideas for new career directions by reading plays and celebrity autobiographies, by listening to "classic" music and comedy albums, and by watching movie legends in their films. You can pick and choose among the show business tips offered, for example, by Jenny McCarthy in *Jen-X* or by Helen Hayes in Donn Murphy's and Stephen Moore's *Helen Hayes: A Bio-Bibliography*. McCarthy writes that she knew she had to do something to be noticed, whether it meant making faces, posing nude, or wearing a designer dress backwards. The "First Lady of American Theatre," on the other hand, chose to overcome her forced ingenue mannerisms by taking classes in voice, acting technique, dance, boxing, and fencing.

Summer vacation gives young actors up to three months to take classes that hone and expand their talents. When I was eight, I learned to juggle scarfs in a circus arts class at Chestnut Hill College in Philadelphia. In middle school and high school, I played my clarinet and saxophone in a West Chester University Music Camp program that included a theatre elective. This summer experience helped me audition successfully for Pennsylvania's district and regional bands (the more auditioning experience, the better). At West Chester, I also had an opportunity to write comedy sketches and perfect my improv skills. Inspired by the hair nets, latex gloves, quivering Jell-O, and mystery meat that were part of our daily meals, I wrote the down and dirty rendition of "The West Chester Music Camp Cafeteria Blues" that we sang in a camp revue.

Throughout the year, young actors can take advantage of the training opportunities offered in school and in their neighborhoods. In most communities, someone teaches dance, voice, musical instruments, gymnastics, foreign languages, figure skating, horseback riding, karate, and more. Everywhere teams are forming to play a wide variety of sports.

Not only do these activities add substance to the "Special Skills" section of your resume, but they also may set you apart as the perfect hire for a commercial, film, or other project. I went to my Phillies' audition with more than my improv ability. I dressed my puppet, Petunia the Pig, in a Phillies' cap and performed an updated version of a routine that I had written in elementary school. If I fail to land a role in a musical, I sign up to play my clarinet and saxophone in the pit. I figure the more I can do, the more show business doors will be open for me.

I found that summer stock interns can quickly put new-found skills to use. When I returned from my first summer in stock, I prepared a non-acting resume listing the new skills I had acquired at the American Stage Festival in New Hampshire. I itemized my experience in three categories: as a dresser and wardrobe mistress involved with cosutmes, wigs, and makeup; as a scenic painter; and as a box office assistant. Shortly after I mailed my new tech resume to thirty theatres listed in the *Regional Theatre Directory*, four called to discuss positions. Hedgerow Theatre, where I once performed in *A Christmas Carol*, hired me as a member of its resident company.

Expect to make sacrifices

I do not like abstaining from chocolate chip cookies, missing school activities, losing a boyfriend, or moving to a city where I know no one. Although I was never one to sit on a couch with a bowl of chips, a *TV Guide*, and a remote, I was accustomed to eating several large helpings of ice cream a day. Through my growing years, the calcium helped and the fat did not seem to hurt. By the summer after sixth grade my height stayed at 5'4", but my weight began to climb. Clearly, I had to be more careful about choosing snacks. I switched from ice cream to frozen yogurt and began scrutinizing the fat content on labels. Our shopping list started to include more apples, raisins, carrots, popcorn, pretzels, bagels, frozen reduced-fat garlic bread, hard candy, jelly beans, and bottled water.

As actors, our bodies are our instruments. Makeup, costumes, lighting, and training cannot substitute for good health. Anorexia, bulimia, and other eating disorders have claimed lives. When Tommy Tune broke a bone in his right foot, *Busker Alley*, the show he was rehearsing, never opened on Broadway. Actors cannot afford to ignore information affecting their bodies. We want to be the healthy Shirley MacLaine understudies ready to go on like she did, when *Pajama Game* star Carol Haney sprained her ankle.

Among all the publications that report the latest health findings, I get the most out of an eight-page monthly *Wellness Letter* published by the University of California at Berkeley's School of Public Health (see listing in Appendix B). Wise choices about vitamins, vaccines, sun exposure, safe sex, skin care, dental care, drugs, drinking, smoking, exercise, and sleep are important every day, not just the night before an audition.

No teen likes to be separated from "the group." I must say, however, that the pain of separation and making up a week of high school tests in one or two days quickly vanishes, when you are the center of attention, responding to questions about your absence for an audition, play, or student film. Yet, some friends, especially boyfriends, did not share my love of New York. Raised in the suburbs, not only did they not want to live in Manhattan, they indicated that they probably would not visit me there either. As traumatic as it is to face rejection at home or in a dorm room, it is even worse when you are on your own without friends in a new city.

Still, that old adage about nothing ventured, nothing gained, applies to all of us, including every teen who grows up outside major media and theatre centers. Just about anywhere, there is a chance to perform in country clubs, comedy clubs, dinner theatres, senior centers, community theatres, tourist attractions, hotels, schools, and local radio and television stations. Given the comfort of nearby family and friends, young actors may decide to gain experience and confidence by first exploring these local venues.

The trick is knowing when you have outgrown your little pond and should leave to compete in the big time. When I moved to New York, actors who have continued to work in their communities into their thirties asked if they could stay with me and use my address as they tried their luck in the city. They knew that they should be near Broadway, and yet they were reluctant to make the sacrifices required by an all-out commitment to their profession.

Develop coping tactics

I am convinced that planning for down time, whether it is what to eat or what to do during the hiatus between roles, is the key to perseverance in show business. Although I cannot cite any survey results, I suspect that an actor's down time heavily outweighs time spent performing for pay.

During highs and lows, friends who are not jealous of my success or ready to dump me when I fail are the cornerstone of my support system. So too, my mother has been my rock. Other young actors also say that they have the security of knowing their parents are there for them. Still, parents can be busy and have their own bad days. Friends too may be out Saturday night, when you finally get home at 11:00 p.m. from your very worst audition. Devastating as well is the letdown actors experience when they return to an empty hotel room or apartment after receiving the public's applause.

When I am alone in my misery, a pint of no-fat frozen yogurt and a Muppet movie have helped me through many rough evenings. To be prepared for these dismal occasions, I try to create an environment to dispel gloom. For me this means hanging a picture of my hero, Mozart, posters from past musicals I have performed, and a theatre scene I drew. I tape "happy mixes" of music that can make me smile at home or on the road. My bookcase is filled with photo albums that remind me of good times and friends. I always have my favorite Squirrel Nutkin and Kermit the Frog stuffed toys within hugging distance. I look forward to having the solace of a real cat one day, too.

Belief in God also lifts me out of self-absorption and provides consolation when I am alone. Life upon the stage need not be wicked. Some who have asked me about the St. Genesius medal I wear are surprised to find actors have a patron saint. Others share with me their own devotions and spiritual thoughts. All in all, no one really needs to tell any of us that meditation and running our fingers over prayer beads are much healthier alternatives than the other ways we could have chosen to deal with rejection and loneliness.

Recording thoughts, spiritual and otherwise, in a journal helps release sadness. In this electronic age when messages disappear as fast as they are read, those actors who make hard copies also may be producing the historical documents researchers will use to make them famous. If that idea fails to console, there is nothing like an all-out cry to purge bad feelings. Depending on your weeping style, you may even fall asleep and wake up to a brand-new day. Eye puffiness will disappear before the next big audition.

My first month in New York was the loneliest in my 18 years of life. I called the only acquaintance I knew in the city, and she was busy rehearsing for a play. Although I lived in a women's residence in a safe area, walking around alone with no one to hang out with and having only enough money for an occasional movie were no fun. Three friends from home came to visit, but two could stay only one day. Thank goodness for the telephone and my interest in the World Series. They made my nights more bearable!

Every day I had an agenda. I applied for a New York driver's license and library card, joined a local church and its young people's group, and registered to vote in time to cast my first ballot a month later. I found two of the best breakfast places in the area, a bar that does not card, the cheapest 24-hour diner on the block, and a wonderful bookstore. I sent out headshots, called in response to classified ads, filled out employment applications in person, registered for clarinet lessons at a music school, and wrote lots of personal letters.

Gradually, I began to recognize familiar faces and to have more common ground for conversation. My godfather called unexpectedly to invite me out to Long Island for dinner. Starting out alone, living many miles from close friends and family, is very, very difficult. But every time I had visitors, I felt great showing them around "my new city."

When I left New York to perform in summer stock, I had every intention of returning in September. Little did I know that I would acquire new skills in wardrobe, scenic painting and box office that would make me desirable as a resident member of a theatre company. I guess it is as I said: few decisions actors make are final.

Chapter 12:
Reflections for Parents

Understanding • Contributions • Letting Go

I am not a stage mother, but by the time Annie reached middle school I knew that I was the mother of a daughter with stage ambitions. Annie once said that her school year began when the tryout notice was posted for the spring musical. There is just enough show business blood in my family to help me understand how entertaining could be in her veins, too. As a trained marketer, I also knew that my promotional skills could help further Annie's career.

Understand the young actor

My father was a band leader, before the second world war stepped in with other plans for his "troops." At high school dad-and-daughter dinners after the war, he continued to strut his stuff as part of a song-and-dance team with me and my sister. My mother had minored in drama in college while she prepared to teach math in Chicago's public schools. She was far too practical to pursue a theatrical career. Yet in her 40s she decided to earn a master's degree in speech and drama at Northwestern University, even though she already had an M.A. in math.

Grandfather Skip used to tell Mom and Dad that they had "a house of characters." We did not make fireworks, but we did leap through the living room wearing short ballet tutus the way an actress did in Moss Hart's and George S. Kaufman's *You Can't Take It With You.*

Mom initiated my love of the theatre by taking me to see *H.M.S. Pinafore* when I was five, just before my sister Patricia was born. By the time Pat could walk, talk, and sing, we started putting on shows complete with costumes and tickets. I studied ballet, tap, and modern dance. As an amateur choreographer, I created dances for teen shows and college talent revues. One Russian extravaganza featured "Ivan," a pillow person that dancers flung into the air to simulate amazing jumps.

Whenever Mother would tell me to walk with toes pointed forward or to sit like a lady, her admonitions would begin, "As Sister Leola would say...." Sister Leola had been her drama professor at Mundelein College in the 1930s. She had taught not only my mother but also Academy Award-winner Mercedes McCambridge. Along with my mother, I followed the career of this brilliant actress as she won an Oscar for her supporting role in *All the King's Men,* shared billing with James Dean and Elizabeth Taylor in *Giant,* and gave the devil a voice in *The Exorcist*. We went together to see Mc-Cambridge perform in *Agnes of God* at the Kennedy Center in Washington, D.C.

When she came to Philadelphia to play the grandmother in Neil Simon's play *Lost in Yonkers*, Mc-Cambridge invited my mom, me, and Annie backstage to meet her after the show. Balancing all the voices that rightly remind Annie and me that there is a broken heart for every light on Broadway is the fact that someone we knew made it.

Contribute what you can

My family-grounded appreciation for the arts tells me that Annie would be farther ahead in her profession if she had been born a Fonda. Or if she had been heir to the height, perfect skin, and blond genes of a model, or the vocal chords of Julie Andrews. No use wishing for what might have been! Every child has certain attributes, and all parents have resources, be they time, energy, money, or contacts, that they can use to help develop these natural gifts.

What I could contribute to Annie's goal was, first, attention. In many ways, a young would-be performer is lucky to be an only child raised by a single parent like I am. No jealous siblings or pouting husband act out because someone else has a greater claim on the family's time and energy. If parent and child are late returning from an audition or decide to spend a little more money for headshots, teeth whitening, and a new outfit, no one is waiting at home to demand an accounting. Working together can even bring in the income needed to survive.

Unknowingly, activities Annie and I enjoyed together began preparing her for an acting career long before she attended her first audition. Spending time at home watching television schooled us in the pop culture that now dominates show business. You can see, if you look at our photo albums and home movies, that we dressed in costumes, built sets, and acted out stories.

When I was teaching in Green Bay, Wisconsin, I remember having an Indian tepee in our living room. The hoop skirt and gray Confederate greatcoat in the closet are reminders of Annie's immersion in the Civil War after we saw John Jakes's *North and South* miniseries on television. Plans for one summer vacation included a trip to Harrisburg, where Annie competed in her first and only beauty pageant. Over the years, we got used to talking to each other, sizing up situations the same way, and understanding when to back off before conflicts escalated between us and others.

My positions teaching college courses and writing a newsletter gave me the flexibility to take Annie to auditions from Virginia to New York. Less flexible were public school requirements for the number of days a student must attend classes in order to move to the next grade. Twice we received a letter from the truant officer saying Annie could be absent only one more day. There was an appeal procedure that permitted a student and parents to argue for an exception. We figured we would win an appeal, since Annie was on the distinguished honor roll every semester, but we preferred not to test the system.

Besides flexibility, I brought to Annie's career pursuits an M.B.A. in marketing. I could contribute a trained marketer's understanding of consumers, product, price, promotion, and distribution. What goes into tailoring the perfect approach to an agent is no different than coming up with, for example, the right shampoo, television commercials, price, and retail outlets for women, 18 to 34 years old.

We needed a list of consumers, i.e., agents, and found the *Ross Reports Television & Film* directory. A headshot showed the "product." For direct mail promotion, I created Annie's newsletter. It publicized activities that showed Annie could make money, i.e., compensate agents for the time and effort they might spend representing her. In terms of distribution, marketing principles suggest New York consumers are more likely to shop in Manhattan than Philadelphia's suburbs. Likewise, New York agents are more likely to represent

New York actors than someone who lives outside Philadelphia.

Let young actors live their own lives

After high school Annie made plans to move to the Big Apple. My rational side told me that I should not let her go there alone. On the other hand, I have loved the city ever since my grandparents took me shopping on Fifth Avenue when I was 12. Annie and I had gone to New York together for the first time during the Christmas season when she was two. We were having trouble hailing a cab, and she said, "Mom, you have to call out 'Taxi!'" In response to her method, a cab pulled right up in front of us.

Over and over again, we read Kay Thompson's book *Eloise*, the story of a six-year-old who lived at The Plaza, a New York hotel. Annie always gravitated to books written by Salinger, Fitzgerald, and Tom Wolfe and set in Manhattan. Her dad still tells the story of taking Annie to a party and finding her in the kitchen discussing *The Bonfire of the Vanities* with his friends when she was 11.

I know that Annie is where *she* wants to be. People tell us we look alike, which makes us both laugh hysterically. Annie always has been considered pretty, thin, funny, and extremely articulate. I, on the other hand, always have been overweight and bookish. Without question, Annie is not living her stage mother's fantasy.

Agents and managers claim that they only represent young people who really want to act, but parents cut from the same pattern as Gypsy Rose Lee's mama slip into the system. I have seen mothers who do all the talking—to the receptionist, the director, the agent, the manager, the cameraman, anyone involved in the casting process. Meanwhile, a son or daughter sits in the corner looking miserable. How unlike the approach of Annie and me! She talks; I sit, nodding approvingly.

Annie and I have known stage kids and stage moms who pushed too hard. When Annie was in first grade, we lived across the court from another six-year-old who rarely was free to come out and play. If she was not at an audition, she was overbooked at dance, acting, gymnastic, or other lessons. Her mother would poke a finger at the midsection of neighborhood kids and declare them too fat. Trick-or-treating was a no-no.

One of my best friends had been an unwilling child model. As she tells the story, her mother dressed her in velvet suits and picked her up after school every Friday for a weekly hair, nail, and skin care session at the local beauty salon. By age 15, she conspired to compete for and win a piano scholarship to a Boston conservatory. When she left home, it was for good.

What would be comfortable for me would be a daughter who cared little about her appearance and everything about working toward a Ph.D. in literature. Annie chose not to attend college. I live where I have to be alert for deer running across the highway. Annie told me she saw her first sewer rat when she was walking to a casting call for extras in an independent film at 4:30 a.m. Clearly, the show business world is different than my world. By the time I was in my twenties, I had a master's degree. Pearl Bailey, the lead in the African-American cast of *Hello Dolly!*, received her B.A. from my Georgetown *alma mater* when she was 67.

Wherever Annie lives and works, in New York or in the summer stock community of Milford, New Hampshire, she will face physical, psychological, and spiritual challenges. I pray for her protection, write letters, and call often. Although I may never fully understand why actors go through what they do in order to entertain us, I know Annie will be okay. She has stars in her eyes and her feet on the ground.

Appendix A: Glossary of Terms

Actors' Equity Association
(AEA)   Union that represents about 40,000 actors, chorus members, and stage managers in live theatre.

Actors Federal Credit
Union   A cooperative "banking" institution that serves members of entertainment unions and arts organizations exclusively.

Ad-lib   Synonymous with *improv*.

Advertising
agency   Company that produces a sponsor's print ads, commercials, brochures, product packaging, and other materials.

Agent   A person authorized by an actor to find work for him/her, usually in exchange for a ten percent commission of gross earnings. If franchised by a union, abides by union rules and regulations and uses union-approved contracts. Depending on the state, may or may not be required to be licensed as an employment agency and *bonded.*

American Federation of Television and Radio Artists
(AFTRA)   Union that represents close to 80,000 people working with audio- and videotape recordings in radio and television.

American Guild of Musical Artists
(AGMA)   Union representing about 5,500 soloists (singers, dancers, musicians), chorus members, choreographers, stage directors & managers involved with opera, concert, recital, and ballet performances.

American Guild of Variety Artists
(AGVA)   Union that represents about 4,000 singers, dancers, and comedians who perform in musical revues and variety shows.

Apprentice
          A young actor gaining experience by working (usually without pay) at a professional theatre. Some apprenticeships may require the actor to pay a fee. See also *intern.*

Artistic
director   Theatre administrator responsible for selecting plays/musicals and hiring directors and actors.

Audition   A tryout where performers provide a sample of their talents, whether by performing a *monologue* or *improv*, or by reading from a script.

Ballad   A slow sentimental/romantic song.

Belting   A style of singing that is loud and flamboyant.

Bonded   Term used to describe an agency or production company that has set aside funds—as specified by law or by an entertainment union—to insure actors against loss of any commissions or payments owed them, should that agency or business close down.

Book   1. (verb) To hire or engage an actor to perform. Also used by actors to mean they have been hired: "I booked that commercial." 2. (noun) Script of a play or libretto of a musical. 3. See *portfolio.*

Bookmarking
    Computer method used to identify and quickly locate favorite Web sites.

**Borderless
photo**   Photo that has no white space along its edges.

**Breakdown
Service**   A daily listing that agents read to learn what theatre, film, and television projects are currently being cast.

**Business
manager**   Person—usually a Certified Public Accountant (CPA) or attorney—or firm hired by an actor to handle finances, e.g., taxes, investments, expenses, loans, insurance, lawsuits, in exchange for a five percent (or more) commission on gross earnings.

Buzz   Good or bad word-of-mouth chatter about something (or someone) new.

Cabaret   A singer's act, often composed of selections that have personal meaning to the performer, performed in an intimate club setting; also, the club where singers perform their acts.

Callback   Any audition for a part after the initial one; a request for a performer to be seen again.

**Casting
director**   Individual or company that producers, directors, and advertising agencies employ to find actors for their plays, television shows, films, commercials, and print ads. Casting directors, in turn, ask agents and personal managers to recommend actors who fit the description of the roles they have been asked to fill.

**Cold
reading**   The performance actors give while reading scripts or lines they have never seen.

Combination
Individual dance steps combined into a short routine.

**Combined
audition** Organized event where actors perform short monologues before representatives of many hiring companies.

**Comedy
club** Venue, often a bar, where stand-up comedians tell their jokes onstage.

Commission
Compensation agents and managers receive. Calculated as a percentage of the pretax gross earnings due the performers that agents and managers represent.

**Community
theatre** Groups that produce plays generally performed by unpaid actors or members who pay dues. Actors are amateurs who have another profession and act strictly for enjoyment.

Composite
Sheet showing multiple photographs of an actor in different poses, outfits, and moods.

**Contact
sheets** Sheets showing all photographs taken at a photo shoot. The size of the images on the sheets is determined by the size of the negatives.

Contract Promissory agreement that binds two or more people in a legal obligation.

**Demonstration tape, or
"Demo"** A short, edited videotape or audio cassette that represents an actor's talents and range by combining clips of his or her best work in television, film, commercials, and/or audition monologues; stand-up comedy routines; voiceovers or singing selections.

Diction Art and style of speaking stressing clear and correct pronunciation, inflection, and projection.

**Dinner
theatre** Restaurant venue where a play or musical revue is performed on a stage after a meal.

Director The person in charge of making or interpreting a play, commercial, film, or television show.

**Equity Membership Candidate
(EMC)** An actor who earns credits toward an Actors' Equity Association union card by working at an Equity theatre.

Executive producer Person or company that helps finance a project.

Extra Actor who is seen on camera in the background or in a crowd scene but delivers no lines.

Franchised agents Agents approved by an entertainment union, because they agree to abide by state licensing and bonding requirements and to comply with union rules when they solicit work and negotiate contracts for the actors they represent.

Freelance 1. To find work without representation by an agent or manager. 2. To be represented by several agents, none of whom represent the actor exclusively.

Glossy An 8" x 10" professional photograph with a shiny surface.

Gross earnings Income before taxes and other deductions.

Headshot An 8" x 10" professional photograph of an actor's face, hair, and neckline. Sometimes used synonymously with picture/resume.

Hiatus Time between jobs.

Hip-hop Dance (and music) style drawn originally from inner-city street dancing; an outgrowth of rap music; may include break dancing.

Historical characters Actors and volunteers who dress in period clothes and portray an earlier lifestyle as they interact with visitors at historical homes, special events, and attractions, such as Colonial Williamsburg.

Improv (noun and verb) Short for improvise or improvisation. Refers to what actors do when they make up dialogue and movements for a given situation with little or no preparation—they "write" their scene as they go along.

Independent film, or "Indie" A film made without the financial backing from a major studio or producer; often low-budget.

Industrial film Film made by an organization to train its employees or provide product, financial, or other information. (Also called "corporate video")

Intern A person who is learning while working at a theatre. Some college students arrange to receive academic credits for their intern work. Theatres may pay interns a small stipend and/or provide housing. See also, *apprentice*.

Interview Actor's one-on-one meeting with an agent, manager, casting director, producer, or other person who could represent or hire him/her.

Jazz Dance style based on (and usually performed to) jazz music, with emphasis on intricate rhythms and use of all body parts. Originally influenced by African dance; now often associated with show dancing, as in musicals and TV variety shows.

League of Resident Theatres
(LORT) An association of professional regional theatres formed to negotiate with Equity for contract terms.

Legit Short for legitimate, or professional, theatre. Commonly used to refer to stage work as opposed to other media, i.e., one would refer to a "legit agent," as opposed to a "commercial agent."

Lithographic reproduction
Photographic printing process that uses a negative composed of dots to print a headshot on paper stock rather than photographic paper. Cheaper, but not as sharp as photographic reproduction.

Manager See Business manager; Personal manager.

Matte A photographic finish that is less reflective, or shiny, than *glossy*. Also called a *pearl* finish.

Media Television, newspapers, radio, magazines, and other vehicles that carry news, features, and advertising.

Media kit A two-pocket folder used to provide the media with information about an actor.

Meeting Synonymous with *interview*. In Hollywood jargon, to "take a meeting" means to have an interview, usually with an agent, director, or producer.

Modeling
agency Company that supplies men, women, and children for fashion shows, magazines, print ads, and non-speaking roles in commercials. Usually makes height, age, weight, measurement requirements. Depending on the state, may or may not be licensed as an employment agency.

Monologue
Part of a play that an actor performs alone; a long speech given by one actor. Often taken out of context and used as audition material.

Musical
theatre Performances that use songs and dances to advance the storyline. Includes a wide range of productions, from the Gershwins' *Girl Crazy* to *Fiddler on the Roof* to *Cats*.

Newsgroups
Internet's electronic bulletin boards devoted to various subjects. Computer users type in and post their comments.

Newsletter
A short written report, normally one to four pages, that presents information tailored to a specific audience. Usually mailed on a regular schedule.

News release
A one-page announcement of something interesting that an actor has done, sent to the media in the expectation that editors will want their readers/viewers to know about the actor. Includes the telephone/fax numbers and name of a contact who can provide more information.

On-camera technique
Methods used by an actor to reach an audience through a photograph, tape, or film rather than in person.

Open call
Sometimes referred to as a "cattle call." An audition anyone can attend.

Outdoor drama
Site-specific play with an historical, biographical, or religious theme. A cast of 50 or more usually play in a large outdoor amphitheatre that can accommodate a spectacle complete with battle scenes on horseback, pyrotechnics, crowd scenes, etc. For example, *The Lost Colony* on Roanoke Island in Manteo, North Carolina.

Pearl
A non-glossy photographic finish, also called "matte".

Personal manager
Someone who, for a commission on an actor's gross earnings, guides the actor's career by offering advice about the selection of agents, audition material, wardrobe, contract negotiations, and other career choices.

Photo postcard
A headshot or other professional photo reproduced on a postcard.

Picture/resume
Headshot with resume printed on back, or attached back to back.

Pilot
Sample television show, made to interest networks in buying an entire sit-com or drama series.

Pointe
Describes classical ballet style performed in toeshoes; often expressed as dancing *on pointe*.

Portfolio Sometimes called a *book*; the album or scrapbook that holds physical samples of an actor's or model's career, e.g., publicity articles, magazine covers, reviews, playbills, print ads. Also, a book showing samples of a theatrical photographer's work, for prospective clients to review and decide if they wish to hire the photographer to do their headshot.

Portrait Sometimes called a three-quarter photo. An 8" x 10" professional photograph that shows an actor from head to waist, hips, knees, or feet.

Principal Actor who plays a leading role.

Print work
  A job modeling for still photographs for print ads.

Producer Person or company responsible for all aspects of a project, including the script, funding, personnel, scheduling.

Production company Firm that films or tapes a commercial, television show, or film.

Project Term applied to any venture (play, musical, film, video), particularly while in its developmental stage. For example, "the new Woody Allen project."

Proofs See *contact sheets.*

Publicist A person or company that an actor hires to create a favorable image in the media, or to offset a negative image.

Publicity Media reference to an actor, preferably favorable; sometimes called free advertising because the actor does not pay for the media time and space devoted to him/her.

Publicity shot Photo of a performance or event that is newsworthy, one that the media would be likely to use.

Reel See "demo tape." Originally referred to an edited selection of an actor's appearances in films.

Regional theatre Professional theatres located outside NYC.

Renaissance Faire A reenactment of the outdoor Elizabethan and earlier medieval faires that combined commerce and entertainment.

Representation
  Legal authorization to act on behalf of another.

Reproduction
house Company that uses a photographic or lithographic process to produce headshots and photo postcards in quantity.

Residual Payment actors, models, writers, and others receive when their work is reused, as in "My agent said I'll get residuals from that commercial for a year."

Resume A one-page listing, generally attached to the back of a theatrical photo, which provides information about the actor's physical characteristics, experience, training, and special skills.

Revue A musical performance without a book, or storyline, consisting of songs based on a theme, or by one composer.

Screen Actors Guild
(SAG) Union with jurisdiction over more than 70,000 actors in television commercials and film.

Screen test
An actor's filmed or taped audition.

Shakespeare
festival Theatre company that produces a series of Shakespearean or other classical works, generally in the summer, and sometimes in an outdoor theatre.

Sheet
music Music for a single song, that a singer commonly hands to an accompanist at an audition.

Shoot 1. Photography: synonymous with *sitting*. A session when a photographer takes an actor's or model's picture in a variety of poses and outfits. 2. Film: to film the action; also frequently used as a noun, i.e., "We spent all day at the shoot."

Showcase A revue-type audition where a number of performers each display their singing, dancing, and/or acting talents for the purpose of influencing invited agents, directors, and producers to represent or cast them. Also: a complete play, running a limited number of performances, for the same purpose.

Sides A small section pulled from a script, usually for the purpose of an audition. As in: "Stop by the casting director's office to pick up your audition sides."

Sightreading
Playing or singing a piece of music never seen before. Similar to *cold reading*.

Sign with
To agree in writing to representation by another, such as an agent or manager.

Sitting   Synonymous with photographic *shoot*, above.

Slate   Identification actors give when they begin a taped audition or demonstration tape by stating their names, the title of the work they will perform, the character they will play, or other basic information. Also in film and television, refers to the chalkboard/clapper device used to aid editing by marking each take that is taped or filmed.

Soaps   Serialized daytime dramas, so named because sponsors originally advertised soap powder to the female audience responsible for the family wash.

Stage combat   Simulated, or choreographed, fighting hand-to-hand and/or with weapons.

Standardized patient   Role an actor plays to help train doctors; actor pretends to have a given disease or to be the victim of a designated type of accident.

Summer stock   Theatre companies that stage a series of productions, usually comedies and musicals, roughly during the period between Memorial Day and Labor Day. Generally located in a popular summer resort area; may be outdoors, in a barn theatre, or other converted building.

Take   Each time a scene or commercial is filmed or taped.

Talent   Used by industry workers and executives to refer to actors, as in "Have talent go to makeup immediately."

Tap   Dance in which rhythms and variations are tapped out by shoes that have metal plates on toes and heels.

Theatrical agency   Company of agents who book actors for plays, commercials, television shows, and films. Depending on the state, the firm may be required to be licensed as an employment agency, and to be bonded.

Theme park   Amusement park that groups rides, games, concession stands, restaurants, and shows in sections designated by named themes.

Under-five   In television or film, it refers to any speaking role with fewer than five lines; can also refer to the actors playing those roles.

Understudy (abbreviated u/s)
>The actor who will perform a role if the actor cast in the role is unable to perform.

Up-tempo Spirited style of song about any subject.

Venue Any place of performance.

Voiceover Dialogue delivered by an actor who is heard but not seen.

Web site Internet address where a person or organization posts information for and receives information from other computer users on the World Wide Web.

Appendix B: Resources

Books

The following publications are all useful; * indicates those that I find myself consulting most often:

*Acting as a Business: Strategies for Success
by Brian O'Neil. Heinemann, Portsmouth, NH (800) 541-2086.

*The Actor's Picture/Resume Book
2nd Ed., by Jill Charles, with Tom Bloom. Theatre Directories (below)

*Audition
by Michael Shurtleff. Walker & Co., New York

Auditions and Scenes from Shakespeare
Ed. by Richard O. Bell & Joan Kuder Bell. Theatre Directories (below)

The Comedy Market
by Carmine DeSena. A Perigee Book, New York

*Directory of Theatre Training Programs
*Regional Theatre Directory
*Summer Theatre Directory
Theatre Directories, Dorset, VT (800) 390-2223
www.theatredirectories.com.

Footnotes.
by Tommy Tune. Simon & Schuster, NY

The Glam Scam
by Erik Joseph. Lone Eagle Publishing, Los Angeles, CA
www.loneeagle.com

Helen Hayes: A Bio-Bibliography
by Donn B. Murphy and Stephen Moore. Greenwood Press, CT

Jen-X
by Jenny McCarthy, with Neal Karlen. Harper Collins, NY

Leading with My Chin
by Jay Leno, with Bill Zehme. Harper Collins, NY

Letters of a Nation
Edited by Andrew Carroll. Kodansha International, New York.

Model: The Ugly Business of Beautiful Women.
by Michael Gross. Warner Books, New York.

Periodicals

Back Stage. and *Back Stage West/Drama-Logue*
P. O. Box 5017, Brentwood, TN 37024-9769 (615) 377-3322.

Weekly newspaper for each coast, with instructive feature articles, casting notices, and ads for professional services. For other cities, see *PerformInk, N.E.E.D.* & *Call Board,* below.

Call Board
657 Mission St., Suite 402, San Francisco, CA 94105 (415) 957-1557

Dramatics
E.T.A., 3368 Central Pkwy, Cincinnati, OH 45225-2392

Magazine for H.S. drama students, subscription $18/year.

The Hollywood Reporter
P. O. Box 480800, Los Angeles, CA 90099-4927;
(213) 525-2018 for West Coast and (212) 536-5255 for East Coast.

New England Entertainment Digest (N.E.E.D.)
P.O. Box 88, Burlington, MA 01803 (781) 272-2066

The Official UK Guide to Drama Training
Westlake Publishing Ltd., 17 Sturton Street, Cambridge CB1 25N, UK.

PerformInk
3223 N. Sheffield, 3rd Fl, Chicago, IL 60657 (773) 296-4600

Ross Reports Television & Film
BPI Communications, Inc., 1515 Broadway, New York, NY 10036;
(800) 817-3273.

Monthly publication covering television shows and films and the people involved with them. Each issue lists talent agents in New York City and California, along with detailed information about those who handle teens.

Study in Britain
British Information Services, 845 Third Avenue, New York, NY 10022-6691.

Theatrical Index
888 Eighth Ave., New York, NY 10019 (212) 586-6343.

Wellness Letter (Sch. of Public Health, U.C.-Berkeley)
P.O. Box 420148, Palm Coast, FL 32142.

Drama Specialty Bookstores in the U.S.

Call one of these, if you can't find the books you want at a local store. They will ship anywhere.

Act I Bookstore
2540 North Lincoln, Chicago, IL 60614 (800) 55-PLAYS

Appleause Theatre & Cinema Books
211 W. 71st St., New York, NY 10023 (212) 496-7511

Backstage, Inc.
2101 P Street, NW, Washington, D.C. 20037 (202) 775-1488
www.backstagebooks.com

Baker's Plays
100 Chauncy St, Boston, MA 02111 (617) 482-1280

Cinema Books
4753 Roosevelt Way N.E., Seattle, WA 98105 (206) 547-7667

Drama Book Shop
7232 Seventh Ave., New York, NY (212) 944-0595
www.dramabookshop.com

Drama Books
134 Ninth Street, San Francisco, CA 94103 (415) 255-0604

Intermission: The Shop for the Performing Arts
8405 Germantown Ave., Philadelphia, PA 19118 (215) 242-8515

Larry Edmunds Bookshop
6644 Hollywood Blvd., Hollywood, CA 90028 (213) 463-3273

Limelight Bookstore
1803 Market St., San Francisco, CA 94103 (415) 864-2265

Samuel French, Inc.
45 W. 25th St., New York, NY 10010 (212) 206-8990

Samuel French's Theatre and Film Bookshop
7623 Sunset Blvd., Hollywood, CA 90046 (213) 876-0570
11963 Ventura Blvd., Studio City, CA 91604 (818) 762-0535

Theatrebooks
11St. Thomas St., Toronto, Canada M5S 2B7 (416) 922-7175
www.theatrebooks.com

Sources

Source of Classic films:
Critics' Choice Video
P. O. Box 749, Itasca, IL 60143-0749 (800) 729-0833
The Big Book of Movies, an annual catalog, is available for $5.95; quarterly catalogs are free. Critics' Choice also has a Search Line that helps locate more than 70,000 titles now available on video.

Sources for scripts (order their play catalogues):
Baker's Plays
100 Chauncy St., 02111 (617) 482-1280 www.BakersPlays.com

Dramatic Publishing
P.O. Box 129, Woodstock, IL 60098

Dramatists Play Service
440 Park Ave. South, New York, NY 10016 (212) 683-8960
www.dramatists.com

Samuel French
45 West 25th St., New York, NY 10010-2751 (212-206-8990)
7623 Sunset Blvd, Hollywood, CA 90046 (213) 876-0570

Source for Monologue Collections
Smith & Kraus, Inc.
P.O. Box 127, Lyme, NH 03768 (603) 643-6431

Source for mailing lists and mailing service:
Shakespeare Theatrical Mailing Service
311 W. 43rd Street, 2nd floor, New York, NY 10036 (212) 956-6245

Source for video and audio demo tape duplications:
East Coast Video Inc.
1650 Broadway, Suite 1105, New York, NY 10019 (212) 262-0235

Reproduction Houses

These are sources for reproducing your photos:
ABC Pictures
1867 E. Florida Street, Springfield, MO 65803-4583 (417) 869-3456

J. Beninati Custom Laboratories, Inc.
42 W. 38th Street, New York, NY 10018 (212) 869-5149

Crown Photos
1600 Broadway, Suite 613, New York, NY 10019 (800) 328-6752

Exact Photo
247 W. 30th Street, New York, NY 10001 (800) 536-3686

Ideal Photos
155 W. 46th Street, New York, NY 10036 (800) 929-5688

Modernage
1150 Avenue of the Americas, New York, NY 10036 (800) 997-2510

Photo Farm
903 N. Fairfax Ave., W. Hollywood, CA 90046 (213) 650-5446

Precision Photos
750 8th Avenue, 4th Fl., New York, NY 10036 (800) 582-4077

Shakespeare
311 W. 43rd Street, 2nd Fl., New York, NY 10036 (212) 956-6245

Signature Printing and Lab
7073 Sunset Blvd., Los Angeles, CA 90028 (213) 962-8159

Taranto Labs
39 West 14th St., New York, NY 10011 (212) 691-6070
(Has a gallery and CD-ROM of various theatrical photographers' work)

Organizations

Casting Society of America
311 West 43rd Street, New York, NY 10036
606 North Larchmont Blvd., Los Angeles, CA 90004
To inquire about questionable casting practices.

Missoula Children's Theatre
c/o Tour Marketing Director, 200 North Adams Street, Missoula, MT 59802
To request their touring schedule.

National Foundation for Advancement in the Arts
Arts Office, 800 Brickell Avenue, Suite 500, Miami, FL 33131
To request scholarship information.

Volunteer Lawyers for the Arts
1 E. 53rd Street, New York, NY 10022 (212) 319-2910
To request free arts-related legal assistance.

Performers' Unions

Actors' Equity Association (AEA)
165 West 46th Street, New York, NY 10036
5757 Wilshire Blvd., Suite 1, Los Angeles, CA 90036
203 N. Wabash Ave., Suite 1700, Chicago, IL 60601
10319 Orangewood Blvd., Orlando, FL 32381
235 Pine Street, San Francisco, CA 94104

Amer. Federation of Television & Radio Artists (AFTRA)
260 Madison Avenue, 7th Fl., New York, NY 10016
6922 Hollywood Blvd., 8th Floor, Hollywood, CA 90078

Screen Actors Guild (SAG) Branches
455 E. Paces Ferry Rd. N.E., Suite #334, **Atlanta**, GA 30305
11 Beacon Street, #5152, **Boston**, MA 02108
1 E. Erie Drive, Suite 650, **Chicago**, IL 60611
1030 Euclid Avenue, Suite 429, **Cleveland**, OH 44115
6060 N. Central Expy, #302/LB 604, **Dallas**, TX 75206
4340 East West Hwy., Ste. 204, Bethesda, MD 20814 **(D.C./Balt.)**
950 S. Cherry St., #502, **Denver**, CO 80246
27770 Franklin Road, Southfield, MI 48034 **(Detroit)**
949 Kapiolani Blvd., #105, **Honolulu**, HA 96814
2400 Augusta Drive, #264, **Houston**, TX 77057
3900 Paradise Road, #206, **Las Vegas**, NV 89109
5757 Wilshire Blvd., **Los Angeles**, CA 90036
7300 N. Kendall Drive, Suite 620, **Miami**, FL 33156
708 North 1st Street, Suite 333, **Minneapolis**, MN 55401
1108 17th Avenue South, **Nashville**, TN 37212
1515 Broadway, 44th Floor, **New York**, NY 10036
646 W. Colonial Drive, **Orlando**, FL 32804
230 S. Broad Street, 10th Floor, **Philadelphia**, PA 19102
1616 E. Indian School Road, #330, **Phoenix**, AZ 85016
3030 SW Moody, #104, **Portland**, OR 97201
1310 Papin Street, #103, **St. Louis**, MO 63103
7827 Convoy Court, #400, **San Diego**, CA 92111
235 Pine Street, 11th Floor, **San Francisco**, CA 94104
530 Ave. Ponce de Leon, Suite 312, **San Juan**, PR 00901
601 Valley Street, #100, **Seattle**, WA 98109
311 North 2nd Street, #2, **Wilmington**, NC 28401

American Guild of Musical Artists (AGMA)
1727 Broadway, New York, NY 10019

American Guild of Variety Artists (AGVA)
184 Fifth Ave., 6th Fl, New York, NY 10010
4741 Laurel Canyon Blvd., Suite 208, North Hollywood, CA 91607

Combined Auditions

These are the major spring regional auditions. For information, send a stamped, self-addressed, business-sized envelope, in Dec. or Jan. There are a number of other auditions, which change locations from year to year. For a complete listing each year, including dates & deadlines, check the *Summer Theatre Directory* (see page 135)

East Central Theatre Conference (ECTC)
c/o L. Gambini, ECTC Auditions, Montclair State University, LI134, Upper Montclair, NJ 07043

Illinois Theatre Association
c/o Mr. Wallace Smith, Executive Director, 1225 W. Belmont, Chicago, IL 60657

Indiana Theatre Association
c/o Amy Rudelaff, Clowes Memorial Hall, 4600 Sunset Avenue, Indianapolis, IN 46208-3443

Institute of Outdoor Drama (IOD)
c/o Auditions Director, CB 3240, University of North Carolina, Chapel Hill, NC 27599-3240

Midwest Theatre Auditions (MWTA)
c/o Peter Sargent, Coordinator, Webster University, 470 E. Lockwood, St. Louis, MO 63119-3194

National Dinner Theatre Association (NDTA)
c/o D. Pritchard, NDTA Auditions, P.O. Box 726, Marshall, MI 49068

New England Theatre Conference (NETC)
Auditions, c/o Northeastern Univ. Dept. of Theatre, 360 Huntington Ave., Boston, MA 02115

Northwest Drama Conference (NWDC)
c/o J. Kevin Doolen, Secretary, NWDC Auditions, Columbia Basin College, 2600 N. 20th Ave., Pasco, WA 99301-3397

Ohio Theatre Alliance (OTA)
Auditions, 77 S. High Street, 2nd Floor, Columbus, OH 43215-6108

Southeastern Theatre Conference (SETC)
c/o Marian Smith, P. O. Box 9868, Greensboro, NC 27429-0868

Southern California Educational Theatre Assn. (SCETA)
c/o Michael Arndt, Auditions, Department of Drama, California Lutheran University, 60 Olsen Road, Thousand Oaks, CA 91360

Southwest Theatre Association (SWTA)
c/o Auditions, 4712 Enchanted Oaks, College Station, TX 77845

StrawHat Auditions
Application Processing, Suite 315, 1771 Post Road East, Westport, CT 06880

Theatre Bay Area (TBA)
657 Mission Street, Suite 402, San Francisco, CA 94105

Unified Professional Theatre Auditions (UPTA)
51 S. Cooper St., Memphis, TN 38104

Television Networks

To obtain tickets for a network television show, send a stamped, self-addressed envelope to:

ABC
77 West 66th Street, New York, NY 10023
2040 Ave. of the Stars, Los Angeles, CA 90067

CBS
51 West 52nd Street, New York, NY 10019
7800 Beverly Boulevard, Los Angeles, CA 90036

NBC
30 Rockefeller Plaza, New York, NY 10112
3000 W. Alameda Ave., Burbank, CA 91523

Fox
1211 Sixth Avenue, New York, NY 10036
10210 West Pico Blvd., Los Angeles, CA 90035

United Paramount
445 Park Avenue, 6th Floor, New York, NY 10022
11800 Wilshire Blvd., 2nd Floor, Los Angeles, CA 90025

Warner Bros.
1325 Ave. of the Americas, New York, NY 10019
4000 Warner Blvd., Burbank, CA 91522

Housing in New York City

Rates vary depending on single or shared accommodations with or without meals included. Membership fees and security deposits may be required.

Educational Housing
23 Lexington Avenue, New York, NY 10010 (212) 977-9099

Katherine House (women only)
118 W. 13th Street, New York, NY 10011 (212) 242-6566

Parkside Residence (women only)
18 Gramercy Park South, New York, NY 10003 (212) 677-6200

Pennington Friends House
215 E. 15th Street, New York, NY 10003 (212) 673-1730

Roberts House (women only)
151 E. 36th Street, New York, NY 10016 (212) 242-6569

Webster Apartments (women only)
419 W. 34th Street, New York, NY 10001 (212) 967-9000

West Side YMCA
5 West 63rd Street, New York, NY 10023 (212) 787-4400

Vanderbilt YMCA
224 East 47th Street, New York, NY 10017, (212) 756-9600

You might also want to contact the New York Coalition for Artists Housing (NYCAH), a non-profit organization devoted to developing safe and affordable live-work space for performing artists. Send a self-addressed, stamped envelope to:

NYCAH/Brooklyn Arts Council,
195 Cadman Plaza West, Brooklyn, NY 11201

Index